HIGH PERFORMANCE PERENNIALS

LOW MAINTENANCE FLOWERS WITH EXTENDED BLOOM

JUDITH ADAM

PHOTOGRAPHY BY TURID FORSYTH

Prentice Hall Canada

A Pearson Company
Toronto

Canadian Cataloguing in Publication Data

Adam, Judith

    High performance perennials : low maintenance flowers with extended bloom

Includes index.

ISBN 0-13-027034-2

1. Perennials. I. Title.

SB434.A33 2002   635.9'32   C2001-903677-9

ISBN 0-13-027034-2

Editorial Director, Trade Division: Andrea Crozier
Acquisitions Editor: Andrea Crozier
Managing Editor: Tracy Bordian
Copy Editor: Wendy Thomas
Proofreader: Marcia Miron
Art Direction: Mary Opper
Cover and Interior Design: Mary Opper
Cover Image: Turid Forsyth
Author Photograph: Mark Mainguy
Production Manager: Kathrine Pummell
Page Layout: Gail Ferreira Ng-A-Kien

1 2 3 4 5   H.K.   06 05 04 03 02

Printed and bound in Hong Kong

ATTENTION: CORPORATIONS
Books are available at quantity discounts with bulk purchase for educational, business, or sales promotional use. For information, please email or write to: Pearson PTR Canada, Special Sales, PTR Division, 26 Prince Andrew Place, Don Mills, Ontario, M3C 2T8. Email ss.corp@pearsoned.com. Please supply: title of book, ISBN, quantity, how the book will be used, date needed.

Visit the Pearson PTR Canada Web site! Send us your comments, browse our catalogues, and more. **www.pearsonptr.ca**

Prentice Hall Canada

A Pearson Company
Toronto

There's not a pair of legs so thin, there's not a head so thick,

There's not a hand so weak and white, nor yet a heart so sick,

But it can find some needful job that's crying to be done,

For the Glory of the Garden glorifieth every one.

RUDYARD KIPLING

CONTENTS

PREFACE VI

3

EARLY TO MID-SEASON BLOOMS 44

First flirting signs of summer...

4

MID-SEASON BLOOMS 80

The lavish season unfolds...

6

LATE SEASON BLOOMS 128

In lingering light...

1

**HIGH PERFORMANCE
GARDENING 1**

From breaking ground...

2

EARLY SEASON BLOOMS 28

The darling buds of May...

5

**MID- TO LATE SEASON
BLOOMS 96**

Full-blown beds and borders...

APPENDIX A 146

Plant Sources

APPENDIX B 149

Zone Guide

INDEX 149

preface

Not many gardeners will turn down the gift of a perennial plant. Despite bulging borders and limited floor space, there is always room for just one more. We can't resist the anticipation of something new, of flowers and foliage that each day reveal another aspect and a new form. We love the drama of plants—the worry of how they will fare through winter, the concern over mid-summer drought and the jubilation when they come back each spring better than ever. Every garden is a book that we "write" by planting, tending, and indulging in prideful contemplation. There are moments of despondency and peaks of exhilaration, but mostly the satisfying day-to-day business of growth, with a hoped-for happy ending.

People desiring quick gratification most often grow summer annual flowers and vegetables. But gardeners drawn to the complexities of process choose perennial plants every time. There is a special dynamic, an excitement, when plants respond to the gardener's faithful attention and return year after year. And it is a reciprocal relationship. We provide thick organic mulch in autumn and are rewarded with a rambunctious complement of spring shoots. We prepare a lavish meal of compost and aged manure and are gifted with a bigger-than-ever flush of flower buds. Our pride justifiably swells with the tangible appreciation of expanding root clumps, stronger stems, and larger blossoms. We are in a relationship based on sensual appreciation—the feel of stiff and sturdy stems, the scent of foliage and petals, the sight of enhanced flower and foliage color. Year after year, the perennial drama continues as we plant the borders and write the books of our gardens.

Gardening with perennial plants can be a satisfyingly solitary experience. The amount of detail to be observed and evaluations to consider leave little place for companionship and conversation. Perhaps that is a polite way of saying we prefer to garden alone, without wristwatch or cell phone, no radio or neighborly chat over the

fence. The garden can be a solace for the soul, a foreign country where we travel the solitary path and visit plants we have known for many seasons past. And who is to say if the pink bleeding heart is more appropriate than the white version or if corn flowers are a truer blue than delphiniums? Would we want to even hear another opinion? The love of a particular plant is a subjective emotion, and it is common knowledge that one woman's rose is another man's thistle.

The garden of my childhood (which is still the only garden I see in my mind) was for a time the focus of serious territorial conflict. I well remember planting out my grandmother's delicate *dianthus* seedlings (sentimental emblems of her own childhood in Maryland) only to find, a week later, my grandfather had sown carrot seed right through the patch. This was one of several "accidental" overlaps between a man determined to fill every sunny venue with vegetables and a woman intent on establishing perennial plants for sensual appeal. Ever the pragmatist, my grandmother eventually planted several secret patches of perennials behind a large peach tree where we nurtured the pinks. And as proper poles were entirely given over to bean support, we staked the delphiniums with African hunting spears, the gift of visiting Congolese missionaries. That was the only known flash point in their marriage, but it burned bright for a while.

With gardening success comes confidence. After growing many kinds of perennials you may find particular interest in one plant family, such as the cranesbill geraniums or spotted foxgloves. That can be the beginning of a career in perennial collection, an inevitable second stage of plant awareness that compels us to acquire every species available in garden centers and seed catalogues. A new bed will be necessary for an entire flotilla of foxgloves, or a berm must be constructed to allow every available geranium a space to ramble and sprawl. The second stage is a slippery slope for perennial plant lovers, and one we gladly slide down.

1

HIGH
PERFORMANCE
gardening

"I pity that man who has

completed everything in his garden."

ALEXANDER POPE

New gardeners and experienced growers have one fundamental goal in common — both want to see success with the plants they grow each season. Much of gardening is based on experimentation, trying new plants to see how adaptable they are to the growing conditions in your own garden. Inevitably there are plants that do well, and some that fail entirely. Understanding why plants fail can take some time, thought, and research, and often leads to the desire to try again next year. But the reward of bounteous blossoms from dependable plants is what keeps gardeners going when others, perhaps more temperamental, fail to produce. Having a core group of high-performance perennials that succeed every year provides beauty, satisfaction, and bouquets for extended periods while you experiment with other plants.

High-performance perennials reliably return every year and bloom for an extended period, often four to six weeks. They might be the plants your parents grew or that you admired over the neighbor's fence. But their best characteristic is a dependable and long season of bloom. Decades ago, when fewer varieties of perennials were available, high-performance perennials were all-stars in the garden. Now they're the reliable backbone of planting beds with much broader diversity.

Today, when you visit the perennials section of a garden center, you'd be hard pressed to name every plant in sight. There are so many new kinds, chances are you may know only half of them. The good news is there's no end in sight to interesting new perennials. Plant nurseries are shipping them across the country and importing new species and hybrids every growing season, making available a "plant pool" that increases exponentially each year. But while you're waiting for the results on new selections, you'll have success with the well-loved and familiar perennials that are low maintenance and long blooming.

Low Maintenance

It's best not to jump to conclusions about the concept of low maintenance. The term doesn't mean *no* maintenance, unless you want a completely naturalistic garden where native plants roam at will. Whatever plants you have in the garden will require some amount of attention, and probably more than once in a season. But low maintenance does refer to plants with strong and healthy growth patterns, that have no inherent weaknesses or vulnerabilities, and that perform well with little assistance from the gardener. Low-maintenance plants are defined by specific criteria, described below.

Soil Adaptability

Plants that don't have special soil or fertilizer requirements are adaptable to a reasonable range of pH values, from slightly acid to slightly alkaline. Even plants that are not considered adaptable by this criterion can be considered low maintenance when they are planted in the situations they favor. For example, in areas of North America with naturally acidic soil, acid-loving rhododendrons and azaleas would be considered low maintenance. But when they are grown in regions with alkaline soil, they are high maintenance, requiring special soil renovation and frequent attention. For success, choose plants that are adaptable to a wide range of soil conditions or that flourish in your particular conditions.

No Staking

Growing plants that don't require staking will eliminate a fussy job and much time spent carefully tying stems in place. Plant stems should have enough resilience to bend with the wind and rain, then spring back into place. Double peonies with top-heavy flowers will require staking if you don't want them all over the ground, but single peonies and woody Japanese tree peonies, which have strong stems with less weight at the top, will remain erect. The tallest forms of delphinium can reach 7 feet (2 m) and also require staking, but shorter varieties like 4-foot (120 cm) 'Connecticut Yankee' and 3-foot (90 cm) belladonna hybrids (the charming butterfly delphiniums) can look after themselves in the wind.

Pest Resistance

The garden should be a healthy environment for plants and people. Nothing is more depressing to a gardener than witnessing the downward spiral of a once-healthy plant now afflicted with unstoppable disease. Spraying with chemical remedies is not the answer for, truth be known, most plant diseases are natural organisms in the landscape and can't be effectively controlled. Low-maintenance plants with in-bred resistance (like many phlox hybrids with resistance to mildew) are the best insurance against disease, combined with good cultural practices and growing conditions. Providing enough air circulation around plants prevents more disease problems than any form of chemical intervention. Plants chronically troubled by destructive insects should also

Roots of perennial plants are stirring underground in late winter, even while air temperature is still below freezing. These day lilies are among the earliest perennials to break spring ground and aren't harmed by late snowfall.

be avoided. A small amount of insect damage can be tolerated, because plants and insects are co-dependent partners in the ecosystem, relying on each other for sustenance and reproduction. Only 10% of insects are capable of damaging plants, and the other 90% work to protect them. Insect damage tends to come in cycles as bug populations rise and then decrease. But when critters make a complete meal of the hostas, it's time to stop growing them for a while, until the cycle of destructive behavior changes for the better. And it will.

Polite Root Systems and Seeds

Vigorous perennials are every gardener's dream. You want to see the robust energy in a plant as it extends shoots, stems, and buds, telling you it's headed for a season of fabulous bloom. But if an invasive root system is also roiling underground, that could lead to a less pleasant, high-maintenance situation. Plants with invasive root systems march forward with determination, colonizing everything in their paths. That is why one mint plant becomes a mint meadow before gardeners have even had breakfast. But low-maintenance perennials stay within their clumps, expanding and growing fatter each year and keeping to the original location. When perennials have been in the garden for a few years and reached maturity, it's not unusual for low-maintenance plants to sow a few of their own seeds. Young seedlings of favorite plants are often welcome surprises and a no-work way to fill the borders and make gifts to friends. But if the plant is producing enough seed to fill a grain silo, and every one of them is germinating, that isn't going to be a low-maintenance situation.

Winter Hardiness

Plants that are borderline hardy, or at the very edge of their hardiness zone, will require extra winter protection to ensure survival, and that's a job you don't want. Selecting perennials with a hardiness zone rating that extends to colder regions beyond your own garden is the best way to avoid winter losses and the necessity to protect plants. Perennials with a hardiness rating two zones colder than your region are a sure bet to survive winter wind, snow, and ice. If you live in USDA Zone 6 (coldest temperatures –10°F/–23°C), select plants that are hardy to USDA Zone 4 (coldest temperatures –30°F/–34°C), and they are sure to survive the winters for many years.

Extended Blooming Time

Not every plant has the ability to produce flowers over a long period of time. Some have evolved in cool regions with short growing seasons, and their blossom and seed production sequence is shortened by premature frost conditions. Many perennials put out their flowers over a period of 14 to 21 days, and that's the end of flower production for the season. But others continue making flowers for an extended period of four to six weeks, and those are good candidates for a high-performance garden.

Growing plants with extended blossoming capability is a good start to lots of floral display, but you can extend the flower show even further with cultural practices. Despite the complexity and allure of their features, perennial plants are driven by a single goal — to produce flowers that will make seeds. Their first flush of flowers is put out with the purpose of maturing seeds for reproduction, and when that objective is accomplished, they settle back into quiet vegetative growth for the remaining days before frost. But that needn't be the case if you're prepared to meddle a bit in their reproductive process.

Cutting off, or deadheading, spent flowers before they can form seeds will frustrate the plant's objective and trigger a new flush of bloom. The second set of flowers can also be removed before seed is set, and so the cycle goes until either the plant or the gardener gives up. But you will have intervened in the natural process of events and lengthened the blooming period without damaging the plant.

If you're stricken with guilt and think a little fertilizer will help make up for your mischievous ways (and perhaps pump out some more flowers), just be sure not to provide anything with a high amount of nitrogen, the first number in the nutrient analysis. Too much nitrogen can shut down flowering, increasing stem and leaf growth at the expense of blossom production. However, a fertilizer with a higher amount of phosphorus (the middle number) will encourage bud set and that means more flowers.

DELAYING BLOOM

If you are planning to be away from the garden when you expect favorite plants to be in bloom, you can delay the bloom period for three or four weeks. When new growth is well extended and appears just about to begin making buds, cut each stem back by a third of its length. This will delay the budding process and initiate side shoots, increasing the number of flower buds, which hopefully will bloom when you return.

Understanding Your Soil Type

If you're mystified by the workings of soil and thinking of skipping over this section — don't. The growth potential of your perennial plants is dependent on the quality of soil you put them into. Understanding how to give plants the soil they need for a long and healthy life is what makes the difference between rapid growth and slow decline. Learning how soil works isn't difficult or boring. When you understand that the success of expensive purchased plants (or your own tender seedlings) is determined by the quality of your garden soil, you'll want to know more about what's going on under your feet.

We appreciate perennial plants most when they're in bloom or offering ornamental foliage display. But of course they are still alive and functioning in their off seasons, before and after bloom, and must have good growing and living conditions year round. And that means a healthy bed in well-prepared soil. Soil preparation is the most important cultural element for perennial plants. It affects their access to oxygen and water and the availability of basic plant foods, and is also an important factor in reliable winter hardiness.

Recognizing soil types is the key to identifying what kind of soil you've got, and most important, how to change and improve it. We've all read about soil with good "friability," but do you really know what friable soil looks and feels like? That elusive friability has to do with the physical properties of soil structure. Friable soil is wet but not soaked. It should have the moisture of a squeezed-out sponge. It will hold its shape when compressed in your hand, but gentle pressure from a finger will shatter it. When you spread it across your palm, you feel and see small fragments of leaves and roots, gritty

SOIL PROFILES

Most garden soils can be described as either clay-like or sandy. But within those two descriptions are several categories that better describe each soil profile and these are some of the most common.

Sand
Primarily large particles of sand, with a small amount of organic debris.

Loamy Sand
A roughly even blend of sand, clay particles, fine silt, and organic debris.

Sandy Loam
More than half dark soil (clay, silt, and organic debris) with at least 25% sand.

Loam
Moderately coarse mix of dark soil, with 20% organic debris and less than 5% sand.

Clay Loam
Heavy-textured dark soil, with less than 20% organic debris and minimal sand.

Silty Clay
Dense brown or gray clay with smooth texture and less than 15% sand or organic debris.

Clay
Brown, beige, or blue rough-textured clay with less than 10% sand or organic debris.

bits of sand and crumbs of dark soil called "peds." It has a sweet and light fragrance that is the hallmark of organic life. When you dig a hole in friable loam, the soil falls away without sticking to the spade. Once you learn to recognize the characteristics of friability, it's easy to understand the shortcomings of your own soil and how to change it for the better. Knowing your soil type and how to renovate it for better plant growth are the keys to easy and successful gardening with perennial plants.

Robust primulas and violets grow in crumbly soil rich with organic materials. Adding leaves, garden compost, and aged manure each year ensures fertile soil and vigorous growth.

Do You Have Clay Soil?

Just watching how soil behaves can tell you something about its character. Some gardens become temporary lakes for a few weeks in spring as snowmelt water slowly drains away. The "lake effect" is a good indication of slow-draining heavy clay soil, just as puddles in the lawn after a summer downpour are sure indications that the soil beneath is compacted clay. There are several kinds of clay soil, some bluish or mustard in color, and others just a dull brown. But what they all have in common is a dense, hard texture that plant roots have difficulty penetrating.

If you must jump on the edge of your spade to get it into the ground, you're digging clay soil. If clods of sticky soil cling to your shovel, you have the stuff that pottery is made from. Take a wet lump and roll it into a sausage shape between your hands. If you roll it on a flat surface, the sausage of clay can be extended into a long string or ribbon. The longer you can extend the ribbon, the greater the percentage of clay in your soil. The sticky plasticity that allows clay to form a ribbon in your hand will compact into a solid mass of dense garden soil. If the clay is in dry condition, the clods may be more like rocks you can't break apart with your hands.

When clay is wet, water will have trouble finding drainage routes and oxygen will have difficulty entering the root zone, conditions that cause plants to die from asphyxiation. If the clay is dry, its hardness is impenetrable to moisture and plants die from water starvation. Either way, you won't have a successful perennial garden in heavy clay soil. Some gardeners replace large volumes of their clay soil with purchased topsoil or triple mix (loam mixed with peat moss and aged manure). That is a pragmatic solution and it will give a quick start on planting. But soil is real estate and you've already paid for it once. It's always a shame to discard a natural resource, even if your clay soil seems completely useless. You might consider how the clay can be amended and renovated, and its texture made more workable.

But let's not be too hard on clay — the value of clay soil is often overlooked. We're quick to recognize its deficiencies — too heavy, hard to dig, constantly wet, or chronically dry. But we seldom realize it is rich with plant nutrients that come from minerals. The dense texture of clay ties up mineral nutrients and makes them inaccessible to plant roots, but they can be unlocked by changing the texture of the clay soil. Amending clay to give it a softer and more open texture is what's required to make nutrients, oxygen, and moisture available. It may not be necessary to replace your clay soil in planting areas, especially if you can do some basic work to reform its character.

Changing the texture of clay isn't very complicated. Two crucial elements need to be incorporated into the soil — organic material and coarse sand. Organic material, the most important amendment, could be a combination of homemade compost, aged manure, tree leaves, and grass clippings. These plant-based materials will bring biological life to the soil, helping to release the clay's mineral nutrients. Adding coarse sand immediately softens the texture of the soil, breaking up the clods of clay and establishing spaces for water, oxygen, and plant roots to enter. The amounts of organic material and coarse sand should be generous — you really can't add too much — and they need to be dug through the top 18 inches (45 cm) of soil.

This is hard work, but if you do a thorough job and add generous amounts of soil amendments, you won't have to do it again. Plants can be set into the renovated soil right away and you'll have the quick gratification of seeing them take immediate hold and put on a growth spurt. In subsequent seasons you can continue to improve the quality of clay soil by adding organic material and coarse sand to every planting hole, but you won't need to do "the big dig" again.

Do You Have Sandy Soil?

Gardens with sandy soil can frustrate your efforts to make anything grow. Their chronic dryness is death to plant roots, and pouring on water is about as effective as pouring it down a drain. There just aren't enough sticky particles of clay and bits of organic plant debris to hold the sand together and "sponge up" some of the moisture. Plants that adapt to sandy soils, such as lavender and lamb's ears (*Stachys byzantina*), usually have fleshy leaves covered with fine hairs that help to conserve moisture within the leaf tissue. They've evolved in hot, sandy regions and seem to know precious little moisture will be available in the soil.

Although efficient drainage is usually an advantage, sandy soils have too much of a good thing. And if that isn't bad enough, they're also cursed with low fertility because of the absence of organic material and biological life. No one wants these problems, and after years of struggle you might think your garden is suited for nothing but a pile of rocks. But take heart, for although the circumstances are truly desperate, they are also easily remedied. Easy digging is the one great advantage of sandy soil. And dig you must, adding organic material in geological proportions. Garden compost, aged manure, peat moss, leaves, lawn clippings, composted sawdust (but not from pressure-treated green wood), processed sewage sludge products, and even shredded newsprint (black ink only, no colored sections) can all be turned under the top 18 inches (45 cm) of soil. Be as generous as possible, for you cannot add too much.

When your digging is done and the sandy soil is thoroughly amended with moisture-holding organic materials, cover the surface of all exposed soil areas with a two- to three-inch (5 to 8 cm) mulch of shredded bark. Plants can be set into the soil by pulling back the mulch to make a hole. Each time you install a plant, always make sure to incorporate organic materials like peat moss and aged manure into the hole. The shredded bark mulch will decompose in place and add to the organic content of the soil, saving you from further digging ventures. You'll be surprised at how efficiently the soil "consumes" the mulch, so plan to replace or top it up each year. This process of feeding the soil from the surface works well to conserve and hold moisture around plant roots and stimulate fertility. Combined with a regular irrigation schedule, you might find yourself in a beautiful garden — and it could be your own!

SOURCES OF ORGANIC MATERIAL

- Tree leaves and stems (whole, chopped, or shredded)
- Plant prunings, chopped leaves and stems
- Weeds (remove roots and flower heads)
- Grass clippings (unsprayed)
- Composted sawdust from non-treated wood
- Mushroom compost
- Aged manure
- Processed municipal sludge
- Peat moss
- Pine needles
- Cocoa hulls
- Straw
- Shredded black newsprint (no colored sections)

The Secret Ingredient

To prepare a new planting area, buckwheat can be sown in early autumn, then turned under in spring and planted with permanent perennials right away. The "green manure" adds generous amounts of organic material to the soil and gets plants off to a good start.

Veteran gardeners tell soil stories that sound like dispatches from the front lines. Their war with saturated blue clay has left a trail of snapped shovel handles leading toward the horizon. Or there are gardeners with sandy soil so dry and porous, they will shred and dig in cotton bed sheets to create some substance. It's the rare garden that has soft and loamy organic soil growing plants of bionic proportions, and it's also never your own. More likely than not, your soil type will fall within the broad categories of rock-hard heavy clay or infertile sandy soil that won't hold water or nutrients. Some gardens have patches of more than one soil type, and those areas will need to be treated differently. But what's missing from both categories is the single most important soil ingredient for healthy plants, and that is humus.

Humus is not a word taught in schools. Gardening magazines hardly ever mention it. Humus is more of a secret society word, something experienced gardeners discuss among themselves. Most gardeners begin their careers with an interest in plants, and the issue of humus is often delayed until there's trouble with their soil. After much futile effort has been expended on planting perennials in dense clay soil, only to watch the poor things shrivel and die — that is when the thought of humus begins to dawn in the nascent gardener's mind. Well, better late than never.

Humus is the fibrous end product of decomposition. All organic materials compost down to humus. A pile of leaves left on the ground sinks lower and lower as it decomposes, until finally, all that's left is humus, a thin brown layer of vegetable fiber that remains in the soil for many decades. A forest is made lush by many tons of leaves composting down to humus each year and adding to the accumulation of organic fiber in the soil. Small garden compost bins and huge municipal leaf piles produce the same kind and basic quality of humus.

Humus is the life-support system of soil, forming a web-like structure of vegetable fiber that gives soil a spongy soft texture. It holds soil together in a cohesive mass, full of minerals in tiny particles of sand, silt, and clay; fragments of organic debris (like leaves, stems, and plant parts); and spaces between for the movement of air and water. Humus creates a friendly home environment for the soil microorganisms that process mineral nutrients into plant foods. It promotes the life of ants and ground beetles that feed on insect larvae, and beneficial nematodes that parasitize white grubs in lawns. The more humus present in garden soil, the fewer insect and disease problems for the gardener to contend with.

Every bit of organic material added to your soil is digested by worms and microbes, releasing nutrients to plants and leaving a small deposit of humus. This is like banking gold under your feet, for each bit of humus adds to soil value in a permanent way. All humus has a lasting effect in the soil for quite a long time, and some kinds of humus can remain useful for hundreds of years. Humus in soil works like gluten in bread, spreading a web structure throughout the mass and giving it shape, form, and texture. Without enough humus, the small particles of clay soil collapse and compact, trapping water within or keeping it out. Humus helps to separate the dense soil particles, opens up pathways for water to drain, and creates air spaces for oxygen. Conversely, without adequate humus, the large particles of sandy soil fall apart and rapidly drain water and nutrients away from plant roots. Humus binds the sandy particles together, forming a structure to hold water and nutrients in the root zone.

Humus is made in the easiest possible way, by allowing organic material to decompose in the soil. Organic mulch such as shredded leaves or shredded bark spread over the soil surface decomposes more slowly, but also turns into humus. Instead of sweeping up every last leaf in autumn, allow half of them to remain on areas of bare soil in planting beds, spread over the roots of trees and gathered around the bases of shrubs. One inch (2.5 cm) of shredded leaves spread over the lawn will settle between the blades and improve the soil below. In time, with the assistance of earthworms and an army of soil microbes, the leaves will be processed into finished humus. It's a silent, economical, and efficient process of acquiring something of great value, and with no cost to the gardener.

If you make your own garden compost, the finished product is rich in natural humus. And if you would like to spend some money, peat moss and rotted manure sold in bags are also good sources of humus. But the very best humus is made from plant parts found in the garden, and that is mostly tree leaves. Composted leaves are called leaf mold and are an important source of humus. The leaves can be your own or a collection of bagged autumn leaves from neighbors. Dig them in or use them as organic mulch on exposed soil, with the sure knowledge that each leaf is like money in your soil bank.

HUMUS FOR PLANTING HOLES

Every garden has four corners, and chances are that two of them are obscure and not in direct view. Beginning in autumn, let these be your sites for humus production.

Clear enough space in each corner to accommodate a pile of leaves 5 feet (1.5 m) square and 3 feet (90 cm) high (if the space is shielded by a tree or shrub, so much the better). A pile of that size will stay in place and won't need any constraints or structure around it. A higher pile might require some wire garden fencing from the hardware store to prevent it from moving around. As you build the piles, wet them down with a garden hose after each 12 inches (30 cm) in height and leave them uncovered for the winter.

You can use leaves from one of the piles for spring planting. Let the second pile remain to compost further. The leaves will still be whole, but softer and easy to work with. Keep a bucket of leaves with you as you install new plants, and dig a handful into the soil of each new hole. The leaves are already partially composted and will rapidly disintegrate in the soil, releasing nutrients and banking humus in the root zone.

In autumn, make a new leaf pile in the empty corner. The following spring, use the remaining pile of leaves from the first season, now 18 months old and well on their way to becoming humus. Be sure to get at the dark crumbly layer at the bottom where leaf mold has already been produced. That's the real gold in the pile.

Fertility

Perennial plants have a good attitude about food. They prefer a meal of high-quality organic foods in the soil rather than quick-fix snacks from a box or bottle that must be purchased, carried home, and applied. Manufactured fertilizers have their uses, but strong plants rely first on finding the basic building blocks of nutrition in home ground. Plants absorb nutrients through their roots and send them up to the leaves where they are combined with ultraviolet light to manufacture carbohydrate energy. This thrifty and convenient system, called photosynthesis, requires only that the gardener maintain a healthy soil with an annual addition of organic materials and consistent moisture.

Fertile soil has two important characteristics: it contains sufficient quantities of the basic mineral plant foods (nitrogen, phosphorus, and potassium), and a moist, humusy, and crumbly texture that makes the nutrients available to roots. Most average garden soil has sufficient quantities of the main nutrients, as well as the trace elements that are also important to growth. Nitrogen is the one nutrient most readily leached from the soil by water; fortunately it isn't required in large amounts. But every garden's soil needs replenishment of organic materials that are consumed by microbes and plants, and must be regularly replaced. Renewing the organic content of your soil frequently by digging leaves, compost, peat moss, grass clippings, pine needles, and aged manure into planting holes and using an organic mulch of leaves or shredded bark on the soil surface is a good way to ensure your plants will have strong growth.

But gardeners are anxious parents, eager to provide supplementary nutrients and hoping for a reward of increased blossoms. The key to using organic or manufactured fertilizers effectively is knowing when plants can benefit from extra nutrients and how much to apply. Almost every gardener has made mistakes with fertilizers, perhaps using them at the wrong time and causing winter injury, or providing too much fertilizer and burning plant roots. The basic nutrients (nitrogen, phosphorus, and potassium) contained in healthy soil are sufficient for the daily maintenance of plant growth. Using fertilizers in moderation will increase plant size and number of blossoms, providing they are applied at the appropriate times.

Plants have their own growth schedule to carry them through each growing season, and the time to apply fertilizers is when new growth is evident in spring and early summer. It's important to wait for plants to initiate their own new growth first, so watch

THE BASIC PLANT NUTRIENTS (N-P-K) AND WHAT THEY DO

Nitrogen — Symbol: N

Nitrogen influences deep green color in leaves and the elongation of stalks and stems. It is essential in the formation of amino acids and proteins, the building blocks of plant growth. Deficiency of nitrogen leads to spindly growth and yellowing foliage. However, excessive nitrogen produces soft tissues with high water content that are prone to fungus diseases and frost damage. Too much nitrogen favors stem and leaf growth at the expense of buds, flowers, and fruits. High concentrations of nitrogen can also induce potassium deficiency.

Phosphorus — Symbol: P

Phosphorus influences root growth and bud set. It is essential to the process of manufacturing carbohydrate plant food in the process of photosynthesis. Phosphorus plays a strong role in the formation of nucleic acids and other energy-carrying molecules, and is important to carbohydrate metabolism and how plants are able to absorb and use nutrients. Phosphorus deficiency results in poor root growth; bluish, bronzed, or purple leaves; and poor bud set, ripening, and seed set. Phosphorus can be applied to the soil by using bonemeal, which contains a particularly high percentage.

Potassium — Symbol: K

Potassium is the most abundant of the major nutrients in green tissues and is important to plant health and disease prevention. It influences strong cell walls, rigid stems, and resilient flowers and fruits. Potassium deficiency causes floppy stems, poor root growth, and a characteristic red or purple coloration of the foliage. Growing tips of stems are especially affected, and flower and fruit formation is poor.

for breaking buds, lengthening shoots, and expanding plant clumps and crowns. Trying to rush plants by providing fertilizer before new growth is evident endangers their performance and life span. Plants begin to grow in response to rising spring soil and air temperatures that trigger growth hormones, called auxins. Trying to force the trigger with an early jolt of supplemental nutrients is like driving a car with the emergency brake on. You might be able to move it forward, but there will be serious internal damage.

Fertilizers can safely be applied in May, just after plants initiate growth, and then again six weeks later. Applying fertilizers after the end of July interferes with the process of maturing and hardening new root and crown tissue, and forces tender growth that will be vulnerable to winter damage. Whatever form of fertilizer you select, either organic or manufactured, pay careful attention to the numbers on the package. They represent the percentage of the three major nutrients contained in the package. If the numbers (sometimes referred to as the analysis) are 8-12-3, the fertilizer is 8% nitrogen, 12% phosphorus, and 3% potassium. The remaining 77% of the contents in a dry granular fertilizer is a filler or carrier for the nutrients.

Water-soluble fertilizer crystals are easy to mix and apply, but plants absorb relatively little of the nutrients — possibly as low as 10% — and the larger part of the mixture runs away from the root zone. Dry granular fertilizers are gently mixed with a trowel or hand fork into soil surrounding the plant (involving a bit more effort and time than applying liquid) and will stay in the root zone longer as nutrients are leached out by soil moisture.

Fertilizers with higher numbers in the analysis are more expensive to purchase, and the price reflects the larger volume of nutrient products contained in the package. But this isn't a time to splurge on a rich meal. Plants can be seriously overfed, sometimes with disastrous results, when repeatedly given fertilizers with high numbers like 20-20-20. High amounts of nitrogen can burn plant roots, setting back spring growth and sacrificing potential bloom. And when fed such a rich amount of nutrients, plants are forced to interrupt important biological sequences such as seed production and disease resistance, and direct all energy toward rapid growth. If you have already purchased fertilizer with a high number analysis, use it sparingly at half the recommended rate.

Perhaps the most convincing reason for being conservative with supplemental nutrients is that excessive nitrogen develops soft green tissue with lowered disease resistance and encourages the growth of leaves and stems — all at the expense of buds and flowers. The desire for the maximum number of flowers from each plant is reason enough to use fertilizers with low numbers all below 15. Garden greed is sometimes a useful instinct.

Light Requirements

Sunlight provides the ultraviolet rays that are essential to plant growth and flower production. It's often assumed that perennials require as much light as possible. If that were true there would be no ferny glades, no shady bowers, no sylvan dells where the cowslips grow. Plants that have evolved for thousands of years in particular locations, such as woodland or mountain ridge, will develop capabilities to thrive in similar light circumstances. Low shrubs from stony alpine slopes adapt well to sunny hillsides in full sun. Woodland ramblers growing under tree canopies are at home in a shady urban garden. The strategy is to match the plant with the available light quality, and that means you must understand the light in your garden.

Measuring the light in your garden is easy if the sun shines into every corner all day long. But when trees and structures get in the way for a portion of the day, you have more than one kind of light. Full sun refers to positions that receive six hours or more of direct sunlight each day. Partial shade is sunlight for three to five hours. Less than three hours of direct sunlight might be dappled shade with some sunlight. Bright shade locations receive no direct sunlight, but have such an open location that bright light, referred to as sky-shine, is reflected from the sky. And of course anything less than this is consistently dimmer and darker.

Shade conditions

Shade is not a curse on the garden. In fact, almost any degree of shade is preferable to the environmental difficulties of full sun. But if you feel disappointment in your shade conditions, that probably has something to do with the impossibility of growing the big bloomers. Expectation has a lot to do with satisfaction. You may have enough light to generate only six blossoms on a favorite rose shrub, and six are better than none. But if your idea of worthwhile bloom is a shrub smothered in hundreds of flowers, you'll be disappointed in the plant's effort. Is the glass half full or half empty? Reconciling expectations with the limitations of the site is necessary if you're going to enjoy the garden. Many plants are at home in diminished light, but none has the disproportionately large and multi-petaled flowers of roses, peonies, irises, and lilies. Many hours of direct sunlight are necessary to generate such generous flowers and it's not going to happen in shade. Fortunately, much that is beautiful transpires in lower light, and with a bit of research and experimentation, you won't regret the lack of those cabbage roses.

First, notice what plants you own that do well in your light. There may be related species or "cousins" that could be found at a garden center. Then have a look at neighborhood gardens and parks with similar light, and you may notice other attractive plants that could also be acquired. Seek out good books about perennial plants and

'Dawn Ansell' primulas are well suited to grow in shady spots. Selecting appropriate plants for the light in your garden is an important factor in growing success. A little plant research at the beginning saves potential frustration in the end.

make a list of those you want to try in your light conditions. This will lead to a bit of searching through local sources, and then perhaps to mail order nurseries. Finally, if you have plants that exist but don't excel in one part of the garden, move them around in early spring, testing out a new location with slightly different light that might make all the difference.

In any shade circumstances, you can maximize plant performance by conscientious attention to soil conditions. Dry shade is a certain killer of plants that struggle with low light and insufficient soil moisture. If dominant trees are causing the shade, they will take whatever water can be found. Amending the soil with organic materials such as leaves, peat moss, compost, and aged manure helps to hold moisture in the root zone. Just as people need a regular glass of water to keep their metabolic chemistry moving in the right direction, plants have the same requirement. Providing water consistently is a necessity if plants are to fulfill their potential.

'Pacific Giants' delphiniums this big require a full sun position in the garden. Trying to grow them in partial shade would result in fewer flowers and weaker stalks. But grown in the correct light, they're the best they can be.

Sun conditions

Gardeners with sunny locations seldom know restraint. They intend to make hay while the sun shines and relish the thought of thick perennial clumps ablaze with blossoms and dancing butterflies. It's an idyllic image, but not always attainable. Sunlight can be a double-edged sword, generating flower-making energy while at the same time draining and burning tender plant tissues. But there are some strategies that will help to offset problems and make the most of the glorious light.

Although you can select plants with strong drought hardiness and an ability to perform in bright light and dry soil, it's smart gardening to consider how to moderate environmental stress. If the garden is drenched in sunlight from dawn to dusk, it would be helpful to install a little afternoon shade. A medium to large shrub on the southwest side of the area will cool the plants down in afternoon and block some of the hottest light. Grouping plants in clusters will form a mini-climate as plants shade each other and hold cool and humid air in their midst. A 2-inch (5 cm) organic mulch of shredded leaves or shredded bark covering exposed soil and spread over plant roots will lower soil temperature and prevent hot sunlight from cooking the roots. And mulch will also preserve water in the soil, taking some of the pressure off your irrigation task.

Watering Plants

The growth of perennial plants is reliant on three simple factors: soil, light, and moisture. It would seem almost any garden could provide these basics. Although circumstances of poor soil quality and low light frequently conspire to skew the growth equation, plants will make an effort to increase their size in less than perfect conditions. Plants can go a long way to overcome shortcomings in the garden, but there is no compensation for inadequate moisture. Water is life to plants.

Stem elongation and bud development are initiated by root growth, and root growth is initiated by soil moisture. The growth of plant roots is informed by a genetic strategy — grow only toward sustenance. A perennial plant will not put roots out into dry soil and will stay within its current root mass, shutting down any effort at above-ground expansion. That means no peony buds, no tall spikes of delphiniums, and no masses of black-eyed Susans. In the absence of life-sustaining water, plants retreat to triage behavior by dropping flower buds and cancelling summer plans.

The answer to this disastrous scenario is to provide adequate and consistent moisture. Consistency is a great advantage to plants, for it allows growth patterns to proceed without check. Checked growth, a term referring to a sudden stop in growth, is usually the first response to erratic water availability. Plants are not electric lights — their productivity can't be turned on and off without serious changes in performance. Gardeners who wait a long time for rain and only water perennials occasionally, when they think conditions might be very dry, are unaware of the moisture content of their soil. Examining the soil each day to gauge its moisture should be as automatic as checking the air temperature for your own comfort. The commanding events of our lives (extra work at the office, taking the cat to the vet, a new bottle of wine) can easily overtake the few moments necessary to stoop down and feel the soil. But losing touch with your soil's moisture content can quickly result in checked plant growth. And the bad news is, plants are reluctant to switch back into growth mode if water availability is erratic.

Consistency in water delivery is partly based on weather conditions. Less water is required in spring and autumn when cool temperatures help to maintain moisture in the soil. More water is used by plants and evaporated in the heat of summer. As well, soil texture has a strong influence on how frequently you need to provide water. Sandy soil drains rapidly and irrigation is required more frequently. Heavier soil with more clay content is slower to release water and can bank it in the root zone for longer periods. Your own consistent schedule can only be developed by monitoring the soil in your garden and getting a feel for how rapidly or slowly it is depleted.

Now that you're prepared to water regularly, just how much moisture should be provided? There's no point in tantalizing plants with just enough water to darken the soil surface and then going back in the house. Many perennial plants have roots that reach a depth of 10 inches (25 cm), and you should aim for "sponge damp" moisture at that level. Dig a discreet hole and feel for moisture in the root zone. It shouldn't be soupy at any level. But soil at the bottom of an 8- to 10-inch (20 to 25 cm) hole should have the moisture of a wrung-out sponge.

And how should moisture be delivered? Water flung about in the air by various whirly devices or oscillating bars powering 8-foot (2.5 m) waves of droplets can be counted on for a great show, but they lose a major amount of water to evaporation. The basic rule is the higher a droplet of water travels through the air, the greater the amount of evaporation and a corresponding drop-off in the amount that will reach the root zone. Keeping the water delivery low down and in the largest droplet size possible maximizes the amount penetrating the soil. Watering with a slow hose at ground level is a good way to deliver water to perennials and explore their new developments in the process.

But if you haven't time to spend with the plants, the next best thing to being there is a soaker hose laid through the bed. Soaker hoses efficiently "sweat" water out in slow large droplets and can run for several hours. They conserve water, avoid wastage, and deliver moisture where it belongs — in the root zone. Put one down and turn it on, then watch for the darkened areas of soil that show you where the water is going. Adjust the placement of the hose to reach your target plants, then slip away for some planter's punch. No one would blame you.

Finally, the single most important improvement you can make in the garden is organic mulch around your perennial plants. A 2-inch (5 cm) layer of shredded leaves, shredded bark, pine needles, or grass clippings will suppress weed growth, lower soil temperature in summer heat, and preserve water in the root zone by inhibiting evaporation from the surface. This is definitely the smart way to garden, and you'll have the gratification of bounteous blooms as a reward.

Basic Perennial Maintenance

Looking after plants has more to do with pleasure than with work, although traditional terms such as "yard work" and "landscape maintenance" don't do much to encourage the spirit of gardening. If you're interested in plants and want to know more about their characteristics and behavior, any form of maintenance will be an opportunity to explore what they have to offer. At its best moments, plant maintenance is a sensual encounter appealing to our senses of touch, scent, and vision. So prepare yourself for a pleasant encounter, don't rush to finish, and allow enough time to do the job right. The plants will repay your efforts many times over.

Planting

Place plants in the correct light. You must work with the light you have in the garden and make good choices in the plants you select. It's best to first understand the available light and then choose plants known to grow well in those conditions. Doing it in reverse, selecting plants and then attempting to change the available light, is more difficult. Pruning up the lower limbs of trees and thinning their crowns will improve the amount of light that reaches perennial plants, but shade cast by neighboring buildings can't be changed.

Always improve the soil. The key ingredient in healthy soil is organic material, and it must be added regularly. Strong plants growing in biologically active soil will consume all the good organic materials you add, so you'll need to add more in a regular cycle of renewal. Allowing a generous amount of healthy fallen leaves to remain on bare soil around plants is an easy way to provide organic material. Also, aged manure and compost spread over plant root systems, in any season, is a good means of providing organic material.

Each planting hole should be improved. Make up a special planting mix in a bucket or wheelbarrow for use while planting. It can be your own recipe and might be different each time. A good enrichment mix for planting holes is 4 parts peat moss, 4 parts aged manure, 1 part bloodmeal, and 1 part bonemeal. Add a generous amount to the planting hole, under and around the plant's roots.

Check each plant's root system as it is removed from the container. When plants have been container grown for a long time, or have just been too long in the pots waiting for someone to get them into the ground, their roots can be tightly compressed against the sides of the pot. If you see roots massed on the outside or if the entire root ball seems like a compressed bundle of roots, slightly loosen the outside surfaces to allow new roots to grow out into the hole. Large thick roots can be gently pulled out or a solid mass of fine fibrous roots can be gently torn to open up the root ball.

Use transplanting solution to water each plant into the hole. Commercial transplant solution comes in three formats. The liquid concentrates are easy to mix up in a watering can; one kind contains a low amount of fertilizer with an effective hormone (indole butyric acid, or IBA) to induce root growth. Another liquid concentrate contains even less fertilizer, but has vitamin B1 (the nutrient thiamine) to encourage quick growth. The third format is dry, water-soluble crystals containing low amounts of

This furry fellow is the kingpin of the garden, and much depends on his pollination services. Spraying pesticides to control destructive pests will also harm the bumblebee and many other beneficial insects, and that is a risk not worth taking.

nitrogen and potassium, and a large amount of phosphorus (the middle number), which also encourages root growth. All three are good products, effective for getting plants to "take" to their new hole by growing roots, and all are safe to use.

Plan to install plants into the garden on cloudy days or after direct sunlight leaves the garden. Planting in hot, direct sunlight adds to the plants' stress of adjusting to the new hole. Simply being moved from the pot to the new hole in the soil is a stressful change for plants. They may experience some shock from having their roots loosened and will also sense the change in temperature from warmer ambient air above ground to the cooler temperature below ground. They will require at least 10 hours to adjust to these changes, which is hard to do in bright sunlight; the whole process makes strong demands for water from the root system.

Dealing with Pests

Watch for plants with problems. Every garden is a special environment with its own set of growing conditions. A strong plant that performs well in a friend's garden may find an unexpected problem in yours. If dealing with a pest problem involves more time and effort than you like, it's a good idea to just eliminate that plant and grow something else you've been wanting.

If you notice insects on a plant, don't panic — they may be good guys just doing what comes naturally. Don't assume there's an insect problem unless you see damage to foliage or petals. If insects are eating plants, consider developing a bit of tolerance. It's not hard to ignore a few holes in leaves and it won't hurt the plant. If the sight of them offends you, nip them off. But if the plant is clearly losing the battle with a hungry guest, it's best to remove the plant entirely. Spraying insecticides is dangerous and time consuming, two factors that will ruin your enjoyment of the garden.

If you notice disease on a plant, make efforts to improve air circulation and hygiene. Trim plant stems back, thin leaves and stems from the interior of plant clumps to allow air and light to enter, and clear up any diseased leaves on the ground. A change in weather, from intense humidity to drier air, may help solve the problem. If disease is eating up a plant, remove the plant entirely. Most disease organisms are permanent fungal residents in your garden and part of its ecology. They fit right in with the place and don't know they're a problem! Fighting diseases with fungicide sprays is a battle you can never win, as there's just too much of the pathogen on the site, and you risk

All a plant wants to do is bloom flowers and form seeds. Regular deadheading of browning flowers can interrupt the seed-making message and keep more flowers coming.

danger to yourself by using the pesticide. If a change in weather, simple hygiene, and improved air circulation won't lessen the problem, remove the plant.

Keep Plants Blooming

Provide water consistently. All living things are dependent on a regular supply of water, and that includes people, animals, and plants. No one wants to have a drink today, but maybe not tomorrow, or even worse, have it put off until next week. If your garden soil is well prepared and has sufficient organic material and humus incorporated around the plants, moisture will be held for a period of time. But plants consume the moisture and some of it will drain away or evaporate from the surface of the soil, and more will have to be supplied. In the absence of sufficient and timely rain, the gardener will need to get out the hose and deliver the water. The important part is to monitor the soil and know when your garden is getting dry. If the soil becomes too dry, plants protect themselves by dropping flower buds, and that is not what we want. You can keep the buds and flowers on the plants by never allowing the soil to become excessively dry. If the soil is dry up to the second knuckle of your index finger (that is, at the 2-inch/5 cm level), it's time to provide water. Be sure to let the water run long enough to percolate down to the root zone. As pointed out earlier, at the 6-inch (15 cm) level, the soil should feel sponge-damp. Using a 2-inch (5 cm) organic mulch of shredded leaves or shredded bark over exposed soil can cut the frequency with which you water in half. If you're supplying water with a soaker hose, lay the hose directly on the soil under the mulch.

Deadhead flowers every week. Remember that plants have only one goal and that is to make a flower and then seeds. They will consider themselves successful if they accomplish that and will shut down flowering for the season. You can frustrate their goal and keep them pumping out flower buds by promptly removing spent blossoms. This technique will add several weeks to the blossoming period and a great deal to your pleasure from the garden. Spent blossoms may look brown and dead, but they trigger an accelerated process of seed formation that spells the end to any more flowers, so remove the brown flowers quickly before this happens. To really stay ahead of plant chemistry, remove flowers when they are aging or fading but not yet brown, and put them in a vase for the dinner table. You'll prevent the seed-making message being sent and you'll have something pleasant to enjoy inside.

Preventing Weeds

Keep the weeds out of perennial plantings. Weeds are not bad plants, they're just in the wrong place, and we don't want them sharing food and drink with ornamental plants we paid good money for. The easiest way to keep weed seeds from germinating and taking hold in the deluxe conditions of your perennial beds is to use a 2- to 3-inch (5 to 7.5 cm) organic mulch, such as shredded bark or shredded leaves (or even just small leaves), on the surface of exposed soil. If the mulch is sufficiently thick, it shades the soil and prevents weed seeds from germinating. The soil will always have weed seeds waiting in viable condition for decades, but eliminating light will keep them in the dark. If something should sprout, it will have a hard time pushing its tender first leaves through the mulch. And if that should happen, the miscreant will be highly visible and easy to pull out quickly.

Learn to weed efficiently. If you are going to spend any time weeding, it's important to get the roots out and pull each weed only once. Weed roots have an extraordinary ability to hold their place in the soil and have cleverly evolved to weaken their foliage necks. That's why grasping weeds by the leaves and pulling results in a handful of foliage with the roots still in the ground. The way to beat evolution is to weed only when the soil is wet, either after

Hoar frost is on the flowers first thing on a frosty morning. While the sun burns the frost off, consider an hour of cool weather weeding. The cool and moist soil makes root removal easier, and you'll be surprised how much can be accomplished in an hour.

heavy rain or by saturating the ground with a hose. The roots will slip out easily with a nudge from a weeding implement. Select a tool you like to use, such as a narrow-blade trowel or blunt knife, and slip it down the side of the roots into the wet soil. Wiggle the tool about and press it toward the root to loosen it, then gently lift the weed out.

Take up cold-season weeding. We are reluctant to let go of the garden in late autumn and early winter when plants are completely shut down, but the earth is still soft and we would like to enjoy some time outside. Weeds are able to grow at quite low temperatures and will make strides in the months of November and December, just when we are without any other garden tasks. It is quite pleasant to spend half an hour in the brisk air on a search and destroy mission for weeds, and our attitude about the task at this time of year is surprisingly different. Give it a try.

Putting the Garden to Bed

Cut back perennial stems and stalks. The plants need to be cut back, their stems and stalks removed, and late autumn is a good time to do this work. It can be accomplished quickly in the cool air, but leaving it all for clean-up next spring is often a mistake. Many perennials begin shoot and bud extensions when the weather is still wet, raw, and frosty in early spring. If new growth attempts to emerge when last year's dead foliage is still in place, it will take much longer to carefully clean the plants without damage.

Divide spring- and summer-blooming plants in autumn, but leave autumn-blooming plants for division in early spring. Most plants don't require frequent division. Some may need to be divided every three or four years, and others might never need it. If formerly productive clumps fail to flower well, they may need rejuvenation by division. The center of large and old clumps can die out, leaving vigorous growth in a surrounding circle on the outside of the clump, and that is also a reason for dividing the plant. Root systems with a central solid mass, such as showy stonecrop, can be sliced into chunks using a serrated kitchen knife or pruning saw. Allow each root chunk to have several eyes or buds on it for new growth. Plants that expand with runners, such as bee balm, can be divided by digging out sections of rooted runners and simply planting them into a new hole. Plants with tuberous roots, such as daylilies, can be teased apart and cut where necessary with a knife to separate the mass of crowns. If the new plants made from dividing an old mother plant are to remain nearby, set them approximately 24 inches (60 cm) apart to allow room for mature growth.

Improve soil texture with organic material and coarse sand. This is a good time to add organic material in the form of leaves to all parts of the garden. Allow leaves to cover and remain on exposed soil for earthworms and microbes to process into humus. If you're doing some digging, incorporate generous amounts of leaves every time you turn the earth. Improve drainage in clay soil by adding coarse sand wherever you dig and be liberal with the amount. If you have sandy soil, concentrate on adding leaves, peat moss, and compost.

Boost soil fertility with aged manure and compost. This is a good time to spread aged manure or compost around each perennial plant after the stems are cut down and you can see what you're doing. Generous amounts of aged manure or compost are all that's needed to keep plants robust. You can also use other kinds of fertilizers during the growing season, but manure and compost are the two most important foods for healthy soil and plants.

Autumn is a good time to divide large perennial clumps. Stonecrop can be divided into two pieces by cutting right through the center. But if you want lots of new plants, take small divisions from the sides. You'll have plenty to plant and others to give away.

2

EARLY SEASON
blooms

"And what season of the year [is] more longed for than the Spring, whose gentle breath enticeth forth the kindly sweets and makes them yield their fragrant smells."

JOHN GERARD

Bethlehem Sage
The Sprinkled-Sugar Leaf

PLANT
Bethlehem Sage, *Pulmonaria saccharata*

OTHER NAMES
Lungwort, Jerusalem Cowslip, Joseph and Mary, Spotted Dog, Soldiers and Sailors, Beggar's Basket, Lady's Milk Sile

BLOOM
April to May

SIZE
Height 8 to 12 inches (20 to 30 cm), width 12 to 24 inches (30 to 60 cm)

FORM
Radiating clump

HARDINESS
Zone 3, hardy to –40°F (–40°C)

LOCATION
Full shade to part shade

SOIL
Woodland, with leaf mold and aged manure

WATER
Consistently moist, resents dry soil

PROPAGATION
Divide crowns in autumn

PLANT PARTNERS
Siberian Bugloss (*Brunnera macrophylla*), Golden Garlic (*Allium moly*, hardy bulb)

It's not very often we come across a desirable plant which craves the shade, but that is just where Bethlehem sage wants to be. Early in spring the spotted green and silver leaves appear and are quickly joined by pink, violet, or blue flower buds that open before the foliage has fully expanded and continue blooming for six weeks. The patterns of silver spots on green leaves are so intriguing that they sometimes distract attention from the equally lovely bell-like flowers. Some hybrid cultivars such as 'Excalibur' and 'Berries and Cream' have almost solidly silver leaves with a green margin, while others are spotted, marbled, and diffused in intricate patterns. When planted in groups, Bethlehem sage is an ideal groundcover that will remain attractive in moist, shaded areas all season.

There are over 100 varieties of *Pulmonaria* that are native to Europe, and they take their name from the centuries-old belief that the plants could cure lung ailments. Medieval herbalists relied on a plant's appearance to indicate its medicinal use. The Doctrine of Signatures was an early 17th-century system of medical diagnosis based on the writings of the German philosopher Jacob Boehme. It reasoned that "God hath imprinted upon the Plants, Herbs and Flowers, as it were in Hieroglyphicks, the very signature of their Vertues" (Robert Turner, *The British Physician*, 1664). From that unique perspective, a green leaf with many silver spots resembled a diseased lung; thus it was assumed the plant would be a remedy for lung ailments. The name *Pulmonaria* is taken from the Latin word *pulmo*, a lung; *saccharata* describes the silver spots as "sprinkles of sugar." Another common name for the plant is lungwort, again emphasizing the efficacious use of the leaves for respiratory complaints. But of course there were no cures to be had from *Pulmonaria*, although many people continued the optimistic belief for centuries. However, gardens were generally improved by the presence of these lovely plants and that has passed down to our fortunate selves.

Bethlehem sage remains attractive in the garden long after the flowers are gone and will stand up to the light frosts of early autumn. Its one necessary requirement is moist soil, and if allowed to dry out in summer heat the plants will wilt and collapse temporarily. Large clumps can be lifted in autumn and the crowns divided. Although some seed is produced it will not often make plants that are copies of their parents. Two

Bethlehem sage is a classic example of the Doctrine of Signatures, an ancient method of matching plant characteristics with human ailments. Pulmonaria's spotted leaves were thought to resemble diseased lungs. Fortunately, later botanists revised the theory and said the spots looked like sprinkled sugar.

older varieties, still worth having, are *P. angustifolia*, the blue cowslip, one of the few plants with solid green leaves and gentian-blue flowers, and *P. saccharata* 'Mrs. Moon', with bright silver spots on the leaves and deep blue blossoms. 'Mrs. Moon' sets more viable seed than any other of her kind, and many welcome seedlings can be expected in her presence. Although most of the pulmonarias have flowers in the blue and pink to red ranges, the cultivar 'Sissinghurst White' is a beautiful combination of silver leaves and white flowers, bringing light to dim places. These plants come well prepared to withstand slugs, the nemesis of all plants grown in shade. The leaves of Bethlehem sage have a slightly rough texture from a covering of very fine hairs, not to the slimy beasties' liking.

Moss Phlox
The Tribes of Tonga

PLANT
Moss Phlox, *Phlox subulata*

OTHER NAMES
Creeping Phlox, Moss Pink,
Mountain Phlox, Ground Pink,
Flowering Moss

BLOOM
April to May

SIZE
Height 6 to 8 inches (15 to 20 cm)

FORM
Low spreading mat

HARDINESS
Zone 4, hardy to –30°F (–34°C)

LOCATION
Part shade to full sun

SOIL
Average, well drained, with
additional grit or sand

WATER
Consistently moist

PROPAGATION
Root division, layering, stem cuttings

PLANT PARTNERS
Lenten Rose (*Helleborus orientalis*),
Grape Hyacinth (*Muscari*, hardy
bulb)

…the Phloxes in the garden-beds
Turn red, turn grey
With the time of day,
And smell sweet in the dusk, then die away…

FREDEGOND SHOVE, *THE WATER-MILL*

Nothing jolts the spring season more than a generous patch or three of moss phlox. Their soft and mossy mats creep forward, spreading like spilled molasses over the edge of a low wall or massing out into islands in the sunny border. The cushiony mats are an endearing shape and soft to the touch, but most impressive are the flowers with deeply saturated color. Each blossom is like a small flat coin of brilliance, and at the height of bloom, the flowers mass together, smothering the soft mossiness below. It is a Technicolor production, and even the white cultivars seem electrified.

Moss phlox is indigenous to North America (except for one wayward species that leaped from Alaska to Siberia) and includes a band of similar low-growing varieties lumped together in the category. On December 10, 1745, a letter traveled by Atlantic packet from John Bartram in Philadelphia to Peter Collinson in London, accompanied by "One sod of the fine creeping Spring Lychnis," the first identified specimen of the wildling *Phlox subulata*. This began an extended stay at British finishing school in the borders of various vicarage gardens, and then on to France to acquire a Continental style. Most influential in the development of moss phlox was Captain Herbert Symons-Jeune, who noted that the plant had "as many little names as ever a Zulu chanted in praise of a conquering chief."

Symons-Jeune was devoted to the improvement of every kind of phlox, adding the vibrant African hues he loved so well to the color range for both *P. subulata* and its taller summer-blooming cousin, *P. paniculata*. The Symons-Jeune Strain was imported back to North America in the early 20th century as a cultivated garden flower, re-tooled and ready to go. Symons-Jeune was tinkering with petal color during the late 19th and early 20th centuries, when muddy carmines and "immoral mauves" were discouraged.

But he was able to develop fragrance in the taller phlox varieties and striking color in the dwarfs. Violet-blue, Bengal rose, crimson-eyed cherry red, and his personal favorite, the glowing salmon 'Queen of Tonga', reflect his love of the African continent. The appearance of deeper-hued "eyes" at the center of many moss phlox flowers is an important legacy of his work.

The word *phlox* translates from Greek as "flame" and is an obvious reference to the intense petal color; *subulata* means "awl-shaped," after the soft needle-like foliage with a flared base. The stems extend along the ground from a central crown, forming an attractive mossy mat with the blossoms held above. In midsummer moss phlox can be sheared back by about half the stem length to

The bright green cushions of moss phlox are almost obscured by sheets of early bloom. Peeking through is snow-in-summer (Cerastium tomentosum), *which makes similar mats of small gray leaves and bright white flowers in May and June.*

encourage fresh growth. Longer stems will root as they go along, a good way to acquire more plants of a favorite color. In the summer, hold a branch to earth with a mound of soil and small rock to encourage rooting; the new plant can usually be separated from its parent in September.

Moss phlox grows well in average garden soil with good drainage. It puts out an astonishing amount of blossoms over four weeks in April and May, with the maximum number of flowers in a sunny location, although it will bloom in part shade.

There are many dozens of named moss phlox hybrids, although a plant simply marked pink or blue is still likely to be a fluorescent color. Some novelties are 'Candy Stripes' and 'Tamaongeli', both white with pink stripes; 'Laurel Beth', with variegated foliage and pink and white flowers; and 'Red Wing', crimson flowers with dark red centers. Two particularly long-blooming cultivars are 'Emerald Pink' and 'Emerald Blue'.

Pasqueflower
The Neglected Plant

PLANT
Pasqueflower, *Pulsatilla vulgaris*,
Anemone pulsatilla

OTHER NAMES
Easter Flower, Meadow Anemone,
Dane's Flower, Laughing Parsley

BLOOM
Early spring, April to May

SIZE
Height 8 to 12 inches (20 to 30 cm)

FORM
Rosette

HARDINESS
Zone 5, hardy to –20°F (–29°C)

LOCATION
Part to full sun

SOIL
Neutral to alkaline, well drained

WATER
Moist in spring, dryish thereafter

PROPAGATION
Seed, sown when fresh

PLANT PARTNERS
Christmas Rose (*Helleborus niger*),
Trout Lily (*Erythronium* spp., hardy
tuber)

If not exactly overlooked, pasqueflower has certainly been underused, and that is perplexing for it is such a marvel of spring. Distinctive in form and texture, with an abundance of glistening downy leaves and buds that beg to be stroked, the warm amethyst, violet, pink, or white blossoms rise 12 inches (30 cm) high from rosettes of low foliage. The perceived disregard may have to do with pasqueflower's ability to grow in less than desirable circumstances, thereby relegating it to the list of plants for rough spaces. Vita Sackville-West, the literary English gardener, had something complimentary to say in *The Garden* (1946), describing the "Lavender petals sheathed in silver floss, soft as the suffle of a kitten's fur…" but elsewhere described the preferred growing conditions as "a bed of limy rubble in the sun." Perhaps that isn't surprising, as pasqueflower grows wild in dry prairie grasslands and on the high chalk downs and limestone pastures of Britain.

Pasqueflower is native to Britain, Sweden, Finland, and Ukraine and was cultivated in gardens before 1596. In Britain it had a strange affinity for university locales, an ironic happenstance, as it had no academic pedigree in Greek or Roman mythology and early herbalists considered it of no medicinal value. "It groweth in plenty…about Oxford," wrote botanist William Turner (*A New Herball*, 1551–68). And 200 years later, John Hill recorded, "It covers with its living Purple whole spots of the Gogmagog Hills near Cambridge" (*Eden; or a Compleat Body of Gardening*, 1757).

What attributes the academics missed were appreciated at the royal court, where the household accounts of Edward I show a huge amount of pasqueflower was brought in to color 400 eggs bright green. (The crushed petals yield a bright, but not permanent dye.) Edward went a step further and gilded the vibrant eggs for the Easter court festival. Pasqueflower has long been associated with Easter, the Paschal celebration, for its blossoming time often coincides with the Christian feast. But there is also evidence to suggest that it may have been a cult plant instrumental in the festival of the dawn-goddess Eoster.

The Latin word *pulsatilla* is derived from *pulsc*, meaning "I beat," and refers to the buffeting the plant takes in early spring winds. Pasqueflower likes a bright, well-drained location and lean alkaline soil that is moist in spring and dry thereafter. It

A well-kept secret, pasqueflower is beautiful from early spring to autumn. Hybrid colors include shades of red, purple, pink, and white, and all put up glowing flowers with silky foliage. The seed heads are feathery ornaments that dry well for arrangements.

seems to prefer rocks in its bed, and stony or gritty soils are just fine, but soil that is too damp will cause the crown to rot. The flowers continue rising from the basal tuft of soft leaves over four to five weeks, and the plum-like seed heads are attractive both on the plant and in dried flower arrangements, and extend the plant's ornamental value to a full eight weeks. Pasqueflower should be settled into a permanent hole and allowed to enlarge itself for several years. Its tap-rooted form doesn't divide well, but a modest number of self-sown seedlings can be carefully lifted and moved to permanent homes. The violet-mauve species plant is very beautiful, and some hybrid cultivars are available — *Pulsatilla vulgaris* 'Alba' is bright white, 'Rubra' is burgundy, and 'Barton's Pink' and 'Mrs. Van der Elst' are pink.

Primula
The Pride of Riches

PLANT
Primula, *Primula vulgaris, P. veris,*
P. polyanthus

OTHER NAMES
P. vulgaris, Primrose; *P. veris,* Cowslip,
Herb Peter, Key Flower, Fairy Cups;
P. polyanthus, Pug-in-a-Pinner

BLOOM
April to June

SIZE
6 to 12 inches (15 to 30 cm)

FORM
Small clumps

HARDINESS
Zone 4, hardy to –30°F (–34°C)

LOCATION
Light shade to part sun

SOIL
Woodland, with peat moss and
leaves

WATER
Consistent moisture, not drought-
tolerant

PROPAGATION
Division in autumn, seeds

PLANT PARTNERS
Wall Rock Cress (*Arabis caucasica*),
Spanish Bluebells (*Hyacinthoides
hispanica,* hardy bulb)

Now the bright morning star, day's harbinger
Comes dancing from the East, and leads with her
The flowery May, who from her green lap throws
The yellow cowslip and the pale primrose.

JOHN MILTON

How sad to think of the gay, but doomed little pots of acaulis primulas sold in January, soon to languish and exhaust themselves in the over-heated rooms of mid-winter. They pine on the wrong side of the glass like a cat longing for escape, bereft of a moist corner in the outdoor world. The primula family is large, for which we are grateful, and it is possible to have various species blooming for more than half the year. The botanical name, *Primula,* derives from the Italian word *primaverola,* a diminutive of *fior di prima vera,* "the first flower of spring." And it is always a sure sign of spring to find the little leaf tips of primulas pushing up, despite lingering snow, on the first day of warm sun.

The most common primulas of garden and hedgerow are the classic primrose (*P. vulgaris*), with loose clusters of simple, moon-yellow flowers that begin to open even before their short stems are extended, and butter-yellow cowslips (*P. veris*), waving 10-inch (25 cm) umbels of narrow key-shaped flowers with flared lips. Both plants are scented and bloom for five to six weeks starting in April. They are the sentimental favorites of the English countryside, and before that were a fixture in physic gardens devoted to medicinal plants. "Primrose tea," says John Gerard, "drunk in the month of May is famous for curing the phrensie" (*The Herball, or Historie of Plants,* 1597). That is good to know, and it is substantiated that both *P. veris* and *P. vulgaris* have mildly narcotic juices used to make cowslip wine and the soothing primrose tea.

Primulas grow well in cool temperatures and moist, organic soil enriched with leaf litter and aged manure. They prefer their soil to be consistently moist, especially in spring when flower production is going on. They are semi-dormant in hot weather, and adequate moisture will keep them from losing leaves and potential energy, although they will endure dryness if necessary, until cooler temperatures and late summer rains revive their spirits. As clumps grow thick, they can be divided every third year in autumn by separating the multiple crowns and setting each one back into the soil. Primulas can also be easily grown from seed sown indoors in winter if a cool basement is available, or outdoors in earliest spring while night temperatures still fall below freezing.

The plantsman Christopher Lloyd grows many kinds of primulas and advises, "Primula planting is not a military exercise; you are not bedding out squads and platoons." That is his to-the-point advice to set the plants into natural groupings and not in straight lines, for they have a relaxed form and don't suit rigid uses. Gertrude Jekyll, a legendary British gardener of the 19th century, kept a primula garden at Munstead Manor that was dear to her heart. The planting was exclusively the hybrid form

of *P. polyanthus*, a result of crossing primroses with cowslips, producing larger-flowered plants with intense fragrance. The polyanthus primulas (which means "pride of riches" in the Victorian language of flowers) were her own strain, hybridized over the years and predominantly in shades of yellow, cream, and white, with approximately 2,000 plants in three large beds. Each autumn Miss Jekyll and her helpers lifted every plant — "All day for two days I sit on a low stool dividing the plants....A boy feeds me with armfuls of newly-dug-up plants, two men are digging-in the cooling cow-dung at the farther end, and another carries away the divided plants tray by tray, and carefully replants them." We can only admire her devotion and advertise for volunteers in autumn.

Cowslip primulas bloom with Virginia bluebells and forget-me-nots (Myosotis alpestris). Could anything be more perfect? The cowslips make stout slumps of multiple crowns that can be divided in autumn when more are wanted. To propagate more forget-me-nots, allow the plants to become brown and shake the clumps to deposit seeds where wanted for next year.

Violets
The Postal Bag Perfume

PLANT
Violet, *Viola tricolor, V. odorata*

OTHER NAMES
Hearts-Ease, Johnny-Jump-Up, Pansy, Cull Me to You, Herb Trinity, Love in Idleness, Kiss Me in the Garden

BLOOM
April to May

SIZE
6 to 8 inches (15 to 20 cm)

FORM
Small tufts

HARDINESS
Zone 5, hardy to –20°F (–29°C)

LOCATION
Part shade

SOIL
Rich, light, well drained

WATER
Consistently moist, water in dry weather

PROPAGATION
Division of crowns, stem cuttings, seeds

PLANT PARTNERS
English Daisy (*Bellis perennis*), Basket-of-Gold (*Aurinia saxatilis*)

Violet is for faithfulness,
Which in me shall abide.
Hoping likewise that from your heart
You will not let it slide.
ANONYMOUS

There are hundreds of violet forms, but the one that everyone knows is *Viola tricolor*, the little purple, yellow, and white wildling of the fields and hillsides, known as heart's-ease or Johnny-jump-up. The cheerful little blooms have long been associated with matters of the heart and were used to treat cardiac ailments and as an aphrodisiac, both of which could be the source of the common name, heart's-ease. Although with what cardiac success rate, and triumph of romance, who can say? Perhaps Love in Idleness is a more accurate name for the potent violet love-charm that was pivotal to the confusion of hearts in *A Midsummer Night's Dream*, and represented "faithfulness" in the Victorian language of flowers.

Viola tricolor has been with us so long its botanical origin has been obscured, although we do know one source of the word violet is *vias*, from the Latin "wayside," where these little flowers are frequently to be found. Among all its charms, the fortitude to endure in the meadows and hedgerows and reliably set seed made heart's-ease attractive to those with an interest in propagating the species. Gardeners on the big English estates worked for decades breeding it with other wild violets, developing larger flowers with dark central blotches that, after 1830, became the chief pansy characteristic. Soon heart's-ease and pansy societies had gardeners and romantics crowding into annual shows of the enlarged and redesigned violets. The spring flowers we know today with rich blended colors and large velvety blotches were developed by 1861 from *V. tricolor* and were classified as 'Fancy' pansies.

The sweet violet, *Viola odorata*, was used by the Athenians "to moderate anger and procure sleep," and by ancient Britons as a cosmetic, presumably for the fragrance and a curious violet glow. The strong perfume of these longer-stemmed, single and double

violets became a commercial success across Europe, and many were named for the *grandes dames* of the day, such as 'Mrs. John Jacob Astor', 'Baroness de Rothschild', and 'Queen Charlotte'. As hybridizers produced increasingly luxuriant cultivars in blue, purple, mauve, and white, the plants were grown and marketed through violet plantations, where they were interplanted between rows of sweet peas and berries to provide year-round cash crops. The Tickenham Hill Violet Nursery, located in Clevedon, produced strawberries and introduced *V. odorata* 'Victoria Regina', a huge commercial success (until it was eclipsed by the French-bred 'Princess of Wales', still available today). An 1883 Tickenham *Mercury* news article commented, "Many hundreds of thousands of bunches have gone by rail and post this season to all parts of the world, for the Clevedon Violets are now a household word. We have been assured on the most reliable authority that our postal bags have been redolent with the perfume of this once lowly, now Queenly, flower and that the perfume crept out of our Railway Parcel Office to the astonishment of strangers."

If given a good start with premium soil, the natural strength of violets can carry them right through the growing season. Violets of all kinds appreciate a woodsy garden bed in part shade with generous amounts of organic material incorporated. The Canadian plantsman Patrick Lima digs a mix of crumbly manure, damp peat moss, and a little bonemeal into each planting hole and follows up with a feeding of fish emulsion. With consistent moisture the plants will produce masses of flowers from early spring to midsummer. Increasing heat will cause them to cease flowering, and that is a good time to cut the long stems back to the central tuft of leaves. Keep the plants well watered, and lower temperatures in late summer will bring violets back into bloom through autumn.

Viola tricolor is a self-seeding biennial and returns reliably each year. *Viola odorata* is a perennial plant that produces more flowers with half a day of direct morning sun, but should not be allowed to dry out. Hardy violets can be grown from seed sown in early spring or late summer, planted shallowly 1 inch (2.5 cm) deep (darkness is required for germination) in rich soil and kept moist. Stem cuttings can be rooted in midsummer, or large established plants can be split in autumn by dividing the crowns.

The common blue violet (Viola papilionacea) *was an emblem of faithfulness in the Victorian language of flowers. Each violet had its own meaning — sweet violet, modesty; spotted violet, watchfulness; yellow violet, rural happiness; white violet, purity.*

Virginia Bluebells
Lady Skipworth's Gem

PLANT
Virginia Bluebells,
Mertensia virginica

OTHER NAMES
Virginia Cowslip, Roanokebells

BLOOM
April to May

SIZE
Height 18 inches (45 cm),
width 12 inches (30 cm)

FORM
Loose cluster

HARDINESS
Zone 5, hardy to –20°F (–29°C)

LOCATION
Light shade to part sun

SOIL
Rich peaty soil with sand

WATER
Consistently moist in spring, drier
thereafter

PROPAGATION
Root division in September, seeds

PLANT PARTNERS
White Wake-Robin
(*Trillium grandiflorum*, hardy tuber),
Spring Vetchling (*Lathyrus vernus*)

Almost every continent has something blue carpeting the forest floor in spring, and in eastern North America, that plant is Virginia bluebells (*Mertensia virginica*). Refreshingly free of Greek myths and unknown to medieval monks, the loose clumps of blue-green foliage with pendant clusters of porcelain-blue flowers are naturalized among deciduous trees, along stream banks, and in wet meadows. Named for the German botanist Karl Mertens, and with a descriptive name referring to the early American colony of Virginia, they are a feature of woodland gardens and "bluebell walks" in parks from Ontario to South Carolina and west to Minnesota, Kansas, and Alabama.

In the rough backwaters of 18th-century Virginia when it was still a British colony, a child was born of Scottish pioneers; Jane Miller grew up to become an adventurous plantswoman. As an adult, the spinster changed her name to Jean, and in the 42nd year of her life married Sir Peyton Skipworth, seventh baronet, the husband of her deceased sister, Anne. Reinventing herself as Lady Jean Skipworth, she moved to Prestwould, a tobacco plantation won in an infamous gambling wager, and set about making her wildflower garden on a river island. Among her plant lists of "Shrubs to be got when I can" and "Bulbous roots to get when in my power" was a valued local discovery cherished above all others — the "blue funnel flower," or *Mertensia virginica*. Thomas Jefferson also took an interest in the "blue gems," and rhizomes were dispatched to growers in England, but the lovely blue blossoms never prospered away from the new American nation (although Gertrude Jekyll did eventually succeed with them). Despite the wave of the tobacco economy and the tide of the American Revolution, Lady Skipworth and her blue funnel flowers rolled over the countryside and happily into our gardens.

Mertensia is a spring ephemeral plant, rising in April and pushing out clusters of pinkish-violet buds that open to sky-blue funnel-shaped flowers with a flared and scalloped edge. They bloom for three to four weeks in cool and moist soil and are especially fetching as they sway gracefully in spring breezes. Gertrude Jekyll grew them at Munstead Wood and described her Virginia cowslips as "a rainbow-flower of purple, indigo, full and pale blue, and daintiest lilac, full of infinite variety and indescribable

Virginia bluebells open from blue-violet buds to loose clusters of porcelain blue funnel-shaped flowers. A near relation is languid ladies (Mertensia ciliata), hard to find but worth looking for. Both like cool, moist organic soil and will sow their seeds if happy.

charm." The plants are showy in the garden and good companions for early daffodils, primulas, and violets. The foliage dies back by June, and the fleshy rhizomes below ground become dormant, leaving the space free for expansion from neighboring hostas and ferns. *Mertensia* enjoys consistently moist soil with lots of organic material incorporated, and also some sand to promote the germination of seedlings. One can never have too many bluebells of any sort and if circumstances are right, you may find little one-leaf seedling plants close by their mother. They will succeed in shady places, and also in bright locations if the soil and moisture are to their liking. Be sure to mark their spot to avoid digging into the rhizomes later in summer.

Windflower
The Tears of Venus

PLANT
Windflower, *Anemone blanda*

OTHER NAMES
Greek Windflower

BLOOM
Early spring, April to May

SIZE
Height 5 to 8 inches (12.5 to 20 cm)

FORM
Individual sprigs or small clump

HARDINESS
Zone 5, hardy to –20°F (–29°C)

LOCATION
Semi-shade to full sun

SOIL
Average garden soil with good drainage

WATER
Moist in spring and fall, dry in summer

PROPAGATION
Seed sown in late spring

PLANT PARTNERS
Species Crocus (bulb), Blue Squill (*Scilla siberica*, bulb)

Star-like they sprinkle
The wildwood with light;
Countless they twinkle —
The Windflowers white!

CICELY MARY BARKER

No one should be without this bright and cheerful daisy-like flower, earliest and smallest of the more than 70 species of anemones. Stronger and longer lasting than its flamboyant and late-blooming cousin, the poppy anemone (*A. coronaria*), the simple windflower carpets the steep hillsides from Switzerland to Greece in earliest spring and, with a bit of time, will do the same in your garden.

Old legends cling to ancient blossoms, and one that has stuck with windflowers is the tale of Venus, who decked the marble walls of her temple with anemones, in tribute to her passion for Adonis (whose name is derived from the word *anemone*). After Adonis was killed in a misadventure, Venus wandered the woodlands mourning the death of her young lover. Zephyr, the god of wind, was able to produce fruits and flowers from the sweetness of his breath and noticed Venus weeping. Deeply moved by her inconsolable sorrow, he turned each crystal tear into a windflower as it fell to earth, and their vivid colors continue to appear each spring in semi-shaded dells and meadows.

The word *anemone* is from the Greek *anemos*, meaning "wind," and refers to the early spring winds sweeping over the mountains and meadows as the flowers are in bloom. The Latin term *blanda* signifies pleasing and charming, so much the qualities of windflowers, with their uncomplicated petals and ferny foliage. In Greek legend, Anemone was a wood nymph who became the bride of Zephyr, god of the west wind. Chloris, queen of flowers, coveted Zephyr's attention and banished Anemone from her court. Ever the sentimentalist, Zephyr turned his wife into a flower he could secretly caress in spring.

Which all goes to say windflowers have been prized for their early, bright, and persistent display, just the thing you will want in every nook and cranny where there are a few inches to spare, or even insinuated into the sunny lawn. The flowers spring from small hardy tubers planted in autumn and will in time sow their seeds and gently spread where conditions are favorable. If you want to help the process, collect the seed when ripe in late spring and sow it immediately, shallowly covered and kept moist. The seeds will germinate the same season and flower in two years. Windflowers need average soil with good drainage and will prosper in spots that are moist in spring and autumn, with a period of dryness in summer. They benefit from the protection of snow cover or a mulch of evergreen boughs. Once established, they last indefinitely in a place to their liking.

Windflowers are charming planted in clusters under deciduous trees

Anemone blanda, *the Greek windflower, is a cousin of the buttercup found in natural lawns unsprayed with herbicides. And that's reason enough not to spray the turf grass. If there are bare patches in the lawn, plant a few windflower tubers there to bloom in spring.*

where they will have spring sunlight, at the feet of woody shrubs or peeking out from the edge of a rock, and will bloom for four weeks if the temperature remains cool. They are photosensitive, opening with the morning sun and closing at night, and are good companion plants with spring crocus and species tulips such as 'Praetans'. The classic windflower is white, and hybrid cultivars include 'White Splendor', 'Pink Splendor', 'Radar' (deep pink with white center), and various blue shades. Tubers are inexpensive so it's an affordable luxury to purchase lots and plant them in drifts and clusters. The dried and shrunken tuberous roots are quite odd and appear entirely without promise of life. Soak them for four hours or overnight and they will change dramatically, plumping up and taking on a sense of upper and lower sides. Look for the slight scar from last year's stem and plant with that side upward, 2 to 3 inches (5 to 7.5 cm) deep. If you can't determine the up side, plant the tuber on its edge.

EARLY TO MID-SEASON
blooms

"Now the lupins have been tenderly packed into round holes lined with manure and 'Oxfordshire dirt,' and we have watered all the new plants, and divided the overgrown roots of veronicas and michaelmas daisies, we are feeling less reproached by our garden. We can, in fact, pause to enjoy it."

CLAIRE LEIGHTON, FOUR HEDGES: A GARDENER'S CHRONICLE

Bleeding Heart
The Lady in the Bath

PLANT
Bleeding Heart, *Dicentra spectabilis*

OTHER NAMES
Lady's Locket, Our-Lady-in-a-Boat

BLOOM
May to June

SIZE
Height 2 1/2 feet (75 cm), width 2 to 3 feet (60 to 90 cm)

FORM
Wide clump

HARDINESS
Zone 3, hardy to –40°F (–40°C)

LOCATION
Light shade to part sun

SOIL
Rich woodland, organic, well drained

WATER
Consistently moist, resents dry soil

PROPAGATION
Root division in late summer, seeds

PLANT PARTNERS
Bellwort (*Uvularia grandiflora*), Candelabra Primrose (*Primula japonica*)

It seems the lovely bleeding heart has been in the garden forever. But not really, for it was introduced from China in 1810 and was a comparative newcomer among cottage garden plants already in the borders for centuries. The plant's drapey blue-green leaves and elegantly swaying pendent flowers inspired a quick show of sentiment from 19th-century gardeners. The British author Robert Thompson (*The Gardener's Assistant*, 1878) declared, "Its gracefully drooping spikes of heart-shaped pink flowers have become so familiar to many as a wallpaper pattern, that further description will be needless." It seems the current garden-décor cult of plastering botanical prints on objects of every kind finds it roots in Victorian times.

The botanical name is derived from the Greek words *di* ("two") and *kentron* ("spur"), and the descriptive word *spectabilis*, which of course means "spectacular" and "showy." The two-spurred, rose-pink and white flowers are perfectly formed and consistently heart-shaped, with such allure that the late American garden journalist Henry Mitchell described them as "clean and rosy and innocent…wholesome, with a dash of the erotic." Well, what can he have meant? Plants that look like objects always spur the imagination to fantastical associations. Turning the flower upside down reveals the possible form of the Virgin Mary in a vessel, inspiring the alternative name of our-lady-in-a-boat. But small mischievous boys have been known to gently press back the two sides of the inverted flower and see — a lady-in-a-bath! And perhaps that is what Mr. Mitchell had in mind.

Bleeding heart is a plant for bright shade or partial morning sunlight. It likes a cool woodsy soil, well drained and enriched with compost or aged manure and liberal amounts of organic material. It is among the first plants to break ground in early spring, the deep purple-red leaf tips reaching out of the ground to cold rainy weather and the companionship of similarly brave snowdrops. This ambitious start makes the plant vulnerable to frost damage, which does occur quite frequently, but only the exposed tips are burned and growth soon continues. The splendid flowering branches begin production early, as the plant is still expanding, and the ornamental display can go on for six weeks if the soil remains moist and the temperature is cool. Grown in

Plants of the Dicentra *family are good performers in shade and wildflower gardens. Bleeding heart's cousins include squirrel corn* (D. canadensis); *Dutchman's Breeches* (D. cucullaria); *and the fringed bleeding hearts* (D. eximia *and* D. formosa).

light shade and consistently moist soil, the bleeding heart may remain standing and in attractive condition through the summer. A stunningly beautiful white cultivar, *D. spectabilis* 'Alba', is also worth having.

Dry soil or too much hot sunlight in early summer will force the plant into dormancy, collapsing the top branches entirely. This does no harm and bleeding heart will return again the following spring, but meanwhile, there is a noticeable gap in the border. Strategically placed companion perennials with expanding form, like sensitive fern (*Onoclea sensibilis*) and cinnamon fern (*Osmunda cinnamomea*), astilbe and hostas will easily fill the gap without endangering the bleeding heart roots. The roots are quite brittle, so dig carefully if you intend to divide the plant in late summer when it is close to dormant.

The term "common" is sometimes affixed to bleeding heart, to separate it from the several other species of smaller plants with longer blooming time but not such big impact. The smaller species include the fringed bleeding heart (*D. eximia* 'Luxuriant'), sometimes referred to as lyre flower for its narrow heart-shaped lockets, like a musical lyre; and *D. formosa*, of which there are many beautiful cultivars including the white 'Langtrees' and bright red 'Bacchanal'.

Campanula
The Tenacity of Blue Genes

PLANT
Peach-leaved Bellflower,
Campanula persicifolia

OTHER NAMES
Willow Bellflower

BLOOM
May to June

SIZE
Height 2 to 3 feet (60 to 90 cm),
spread 12 inches (30 cm)

FORM
Upright clumps

HARDINESS
Zone 3, hardy to –40°F (–40°C)

LOCATION
Light shade to full sun

SOIL
Rich, with peat moss and aged
manure, well drained

WATER
Consistently moist, but will tolerate
short dry periods

PROPAGATION
Root division in spring or fall, and
seeds

PLANT PARTNERS
Avens (*Geum quellyon*), Tickseed
(*Coreopsis grandiflora*)

The European bellflowers have been cultivated in gardens since the 15th century and were wild in the countryside before then. No other plant family is so generous with its blossoms as the bellflowers, sometimes known as harebells, and often associated with cottage garden settings, thatched roofs, and Victoriana of every kind. They are intrinsically natural in appeal, with their nodding stems crowded by classic bells of blue or white, opening successively through the days of late spring and early summer. Bellflowers are compellingly adaptive to every garden situation, and to see them is to want them, whether it be a thick stand or just one solitary spire of blue cup-like petals. Vita Sackville-West said, "One can never have too many clusters of *Campanula persicifolia*," the peach-leaved bellflower, a sentiment with which Christopher Lloyd agrees and says the willowy plant "scarcely ever looks out of place, wherever it may sow itself."

No small measure of the bellflower's appeal is its blueness, and therein lies an enduring fixation for gardeners and trendsetters. Of course there's little new under the sun, and collections of exclusively blue flowers have been coveted in every century. American novelist Edith Wharton's all-blue garden at Pavillion Colombe, her estate outside Paris, was cutting-edge elegance more than a hundred years ago. The cult-like attraction of blue petals may well have to do with their indomitable chemistry, which resists all efforts of manipulation and extraction by plant breeders. Since the discovery in 1835 of red and blue color pigments in petals, stems, and fruits, much effort has been directed to isolating the blue molecule and transferring it to other flowers. Entire professional careers are devoted to the pursuit of this blueness, with intent of transferring it into roses and daylilies. But it has all come to grief. The blue molecule simply will not budge, and one can only admire the tenacity of its genes.

The word *campanula* means "little bell" (from the Latin *campana*, "a bell"), referring to the shape of the flowers. The descriptive word *persicifolia* alludes to the lanceolate (lance-like or strap-like) leaves, similar to *Prunus persica*, the common peach. Peach-leaved bellflower appears in blue and white, and occasionally an old double variety is found lurking in the seed catalogues. The flowers will seed themselves about and each seedling is welcome where it appears. Not to be denied, plant breeders have had their way in some respects and produced enticing hybrids — the pure white 'Alba' or

'Grandiflora Alba' and 'Chettle Charm', a creamy white flower with blue at the petal margins, and the doubles 'Blue Gardenia' and 'White Pearl'. Most notable is 'Telham Beauty', a vindication of hybridizing methods that has double the number of chromosomes, producing a taller bellflower growing to 36 inches (90 cm), with quite large blue-violet bells. The hybrids are beautiful plants, but technical meddling has reduced their ability to self-sow and that is a point the scientists would like us to accept with gratitude. However, we are not so inclined.

The *Campanula* family contains nearly 300 species, some with interesting uses. *C. pyramidalis*, the tall biennial chimney bellflower, has for centuries been grown in pots for use indoors as a summer ornament for the fireless grate. Christopher Lloyd advises to bring the pots in just before the blossoms open, to prevent bees from pollinating the flowers and shortening their life. *C. alliarifolia* is a cunning little perennial with white bells that will bloom in shade and makes a pleasant border for an informal walkway. And of course *C. medium*, the biennial Canterbury bells (or bats-in-the-belfry) are good for shocking the neighbors with their flamboyant display of oversized cup and saucer flowers. All the campanulas are shade tolerant, blooming respectably in light shade and excelling as they come into more sunlight. They want organic soil with aged manure enrichment and consistent moisture to keep up with their long blooming cycle. If the spent flowers are promptly removed, the plants will continue putting out blossoms for six to eight weeks.

Bellflowers are happy to bloom from June to August in small spaces. Their bells are designed to welcome pollinators and perpetuate future generations of blue genes.

Columbine
The Perpetual Traveler

PLANT
Columbine, *Aquilegia* species and hybrids

OTHER NAMES
Our Lady's Gloves, Meeting Houses, Chinese Lanterns, Granny-Bonnets

BLOOM
May to June

SIZE
Height 8 inches to 3 feet (20 cm to 90 cm)

FORM
Open clump

HARDINESS
Zone 3, hardy to –40°F (–40°C)

LOCATION
Light shade to part sun

SOIL
Woodland, organic, well drained

WATER
Consistently moist

PROPAGATION
Seed

PLANT PARTNERS
Heart-leaved Bergenia (*Bergenia cordifolia*), Cushion Spurge (*Euphorbia polychroma*)

Certain plants have no acquaintance with restraint, and columbine is one of them. Although often described as short-lived perennials that are exhausted in three or four seasons, they hybridize easily among themselves and guarantee successive generations will roam the garden in perpetuity. It seems that just the right amount of seeds germinate each year and in charming, if unpredictable places. They are good companions for roses, but are just as likely to spring from cracks in rocks. And this is quite a nice arrangement so long as you are not concerned with pedigrees and parentage, for columbines embrace the first breeding partner they encounter. As one nurseryman puts it, "Their morals leave much to be desired." Perhaps so, but it's not for us to say. We are just pleased to have such an enthusiastic effort on their part, furnishing the garden with impromptu displays of the airy flowers, like so many butterflies in flight over the late spring borders.

Columbines are native plants in cool temperate regions of England and North America, and have been cultivated in gardens for as long as records exist. Listed as a home remedy for the European pestilence of 1373, they also appeared in medieval heraldry as "a branch of Collobyns blue, the stalk vert…" on the crest of the feudal Barons Grey of Vitten. The herbalist William Turner (*A New Herball*, 1551) noticed that the seeds are "like unto flees," and indeed they do resemble creatures that might be found crawling about the dog's neck. Although mildly toxic, they were used for various maladies, as noted in J.P. de Tournefort's *Herbal* (1719): "The seed is in frequent use among Women, in driving out the Measles and Small Pox." This went on for some time until it was noticed children frequently perished from overdoses of columbine, at which point the interest passed back to the garden.

The word *aquilegia* derives from the Latin *aquila* (an eagle), a reference to the similarity of eagle's talons with the short and curled nectaries of *A. vulgaris*, the wild blue or purple blossom of the hedgerows and forest edge. The common name, columbine, is from the Latin word *columba* (a dove or pigeon), as the flowers appear to be a flock of birds in flight. The species flowers of Europe and North America are almost all of similar architecture — trembling blossoms hanging downward with their short nectaries curling up and back. The Victorians perceived each differently and, in their penchant for the language of flowers, ascribed purple columbines with the value of "resolution," while red flowers (*A. canadensis*) were labeled "anxious and trembling"; but all columbines were represented by "folly," an allusion to the resemblance of the nectaries to a court jester's hat.

Many columbines are sweetly scented. The American columbines, *A. chrysantha* (yellow) and *A. caerulea* (blue and white), and the familiar *A. vulgaris* (blue-purple) have a candy scent. The 12-inch (30 cm) *A. viridiflora* (brown and green) has been described as smelling of new-mown hay. The image of fluttering birds has been reinforced by contemporary hybrid columbines, in which the blossoms have been manipulated to face upward, and the nectaries have been extended in a dramatic sweep back. The Victorian gardener William Robinson said, "No plants are more capricious," referring to the compulsive hybridizing that goes on and the resultant mix of unpredictable colors, but usually the results are acceptable. A new form of blossom is found in the chrysanthemum-like 'Nora Barlow' series, named for the botanist Lady Emma Nora Barlow (1885–1989), a granddaughter of Charles Darwin. 'Nora Barlow' is a robust plant with beautiful pink, green, and white blossoms on strong 36-inch (90 cm) stems. As well, there are her cousins in named colors.

'McKana's Giants' are one of the largest and most vigorous columbines, like Vegas showgirls in the border. The bi-color flowers are outward facing, with long elegant spurs flying behind.

Columbines are plants of the cool and shady borders, prospering in light shade to partial sunlight and moist, organic soil. They are among the first plants to emerge in spring and can be counted on to extend their blooming period for five to six weeks, but when grown in too much strong sun they will quickly get on to seeding. The nectaries swell with seeds when the flowers are finished and can be cut for dried indoor arrangements before the seed is spilled. Columbines are some-times bothered by a leaf miner that chews circular tunnels inside the upper and lower leaf surfaces, and if that is apparent, pick off affected leaves quickly. The Canadian plantsman Patrick Lima reports that *A. alpina* 'Hensol Harebell', with blue flowers on a 3-foot (90 cm) plant, appears to be immune to the attentions of chewing insects.

Cottage Pinks
"The Bosomes of the Beautiful"

PLANT
Cottage Pinks, *Dianthus plumarius*

OTHER NAMES
Grass Pink, Scotch Pink,
Pheasant's-eye Pink, Gillyflowers,
Sops in Wine, Small Honesties

BLOOM
May to July

SIZE
Height to 12 inches (30 cm), width
12 inches (30 cm)

FORM
Dense mound

HARDINESS
Zone 4, hardy to –30°F (–34°C)

LOCATION
Part shade to full sun

SOIL
Well-drained, neutral to alkaline soil

WATER
Consistently moist, will tolerate
short drought

PROPAGATION
Seeds, summer stem cuttings,
layering, and root division in spring

PLANT PARTNERS
Cupid's Dart (*Catananche caerulea*),
Sundrops (*Oenothera tetragona*)

The British are mad for pinks and carnations, and have been so for hundreds of years. There is no reasoning with them over these little flowers, which are very charming and fragrant, and appear in so many petal forms and colors. They are just the thing to make a delicate skirt on one side of a massive boulder, or flow out and over the top of a stone retaining wall. They come to us with strong references. William Cobbett, the 18th-century firebrand social critic (on both sides of the Atlantic Ocean), instantly dropped his tough radical stance when addressing the issue of dianthus, saying, "For my part…I hesitate not a moment to prefer the plant of a fine carnation, to a gold watch set with diamonds." Now that is an endorsement to consider.

Pinks are thought to be the gift of Jove and their name is made up of the Greek words *dios*, "divine," and *anthos*, "flower," indicating Jove's flower or a divine flower. They have crept about the British Isles for so many hundred of years, there is no definitive acknowledgment of their source. But some believe pinks were discovered in Spain in the days of Augustus Caesar and came to Britain at the time of the Norman Conquest, concealed in a shipment of stone imported by the Normans for building. The flowers instantly seized the attention of commoners and noblemen, who grew them in every available nook and cranny, attaching such fanciful names to hybrids as 'The Bleeding Swain', 'The Duchess of Hamilton's Pride', and 'The Fiery Trial'. Needless to say, great rivalries existed between growers and exhibitors, and competitive displays could as easily end in a pitched battle as in the tea and biscuit tent.

Cottage pinks, *D. plumarius*, form a dense mound of narrow evergreen leaves with fringed and scented flowers in rose, pink, or bi-color on 12-inch (30 cm) stems. The flowers have characteristic ragged edges, or "pinking," which is where we acquired the concept of decorated or "pinked" edges in sewing fabric (and from which we invented pinking shears). But pink as a color didn't exist until the 18th century and probably

▶ *The love of pinks keeps British gardeners out in the noonday sun. Cheddar pinks,* Dianthus gratianopolitanus, *are part of a big tribe of attractive gray-green clumps blooming from May to July.*

was taken from the shades of dianthus petals. Pinks love limey soils with lots of coarse sand incorporated for drainage and make good plants for bordering stone walkways or growing among rocks in the perennial border where these conditions are likely to exist. Cottage pinks grow best in full sun and cool northern summers. 'Allwoodii' pinks are a cousin with the same compact form and inherited wide range of colors from carnations, including velvet black-red ('Ian') and deep salmon ('Doris'), and they prefer a warmer climate in part shade. The British author William Robinson (*The British Flower Garden*, 1883) was fond of Cheddar pinks (*D. gratianopolitanus*), a low and dense matting variety found naturalized on the rocks at Cheddar in Somerset. He reasoned they would be "quite happy on an old wall.…To establish it on the top of, or any part of an old wall, sow the seed on the wall in a little cushion of Moss, if such exists, or, if not, place a little earth in a chink with the seed." And it still works, if the process takes place in spring and we remember to provide water for the little seedlings as they poke out. A modern cultivar of Cheddar pinks is 'Tiny Rubies', which makes a 4-inch (10 cm) mounded mat of sweet grass-green foliage smothered in intensely rose-pink tiny flowers with a rich clove-like fragrance.

Pinks became one of the important seven florists' flowers, the others being the auricula, polyanthus, hyacinth, tulip, anemone, and ranunculus, and they were bred with obsessive attention to detail. The ideal flower was single with a dark eye, a perfect circle of petals with none overlapping, and a smooth flat surface with no fringing on the petal edges. Fringing was thought to be an unnecessary affectation favored by the working classes, a distinction that could only have been made in Britain, where even flowers have their place in the class system. In North America we also associate dianthus carnations with florists' flowers and have been so vulgar as to dye them green on St. Patrick's Day. Gerard points out, "These plants are not used either in meate or medecine, but esteemed for their beautie to deck up gardens, the bosomes of the beautifull, garlands and crownes for pleasure." Indeed, the flowers were symbolic of marital bliss and it was a rural custom to hide a carnation in the bridal petticoats and send the groom scurrying after it (for which he showed little reluctance), a custom we see extended to the ceremony of bridal garters in this century. So it must be the purest form of love between the British and these little gillyflowers that have no other purpose than to preoccupy noble men and ladies, and amuse the country folk.

Daylily
The Plant of Forgetfulness

And the wandlike lily which lifted up,
As a Maenad, its moonlight-colored cup,
Till the fiery star, which is its eye,
Gazed through clear dew on the tender sky.

PERCY BYSSHE SHELLEY

Every plant has its requirements, certain small or large points of order to its universe, which must be in place for anything meaningful to happen. But there is one exception, and that is daylilies, which expect very little for their services and seem willing to perform in the widest possible range of circumstances. The American gardener Louise Beebe Wilder said, "It is the mission, or perhaps we should say the destiny, of certain plants…to make the world in which they live a pleasanter and more gracious place," which adequately sums up the selfless performance of daylilies in the garden and along the roadside.

Hybrid daylily catalogues take their place alongside science fiction these days, and it's a long while since anyone can remember seeing an uncomplicated and unadorned flower. Modern hybrids are diploid, triploid, or tetraploid, the new vocabulary indicating the increase of chromosomes in each variety and the complex instructions carried therein. Would you like your daylily blossoms with piecrust (crimped and ruffled petal edges) or watermarks (deeply stained demarcation at the throat)? Will you settle for one season of bloom, or would you prefer a second bloom in late summer? And do you require a mini-plant under 10 inches (25 cm), or something able to reach 5 feet (150 cm)? It seems daylilies have gone the way of corn, with their genes pushed about and foreign matter spliced in. But no one ever saw a daylily anything less than beautiful, so we must not be too critical of those who gild the lily.

The tawny daylily, *H. fulva*, is the orange-flowering plant everyone knows from country roadsides. It was called *Hsuan T'sao* or the Plant of Forgetfulness in China, where it was cultivated at a very early date and was thought to cure sorrow by causing

PLANT
Daylily, *Hemerocallis* spp.

OTHER NAMES
Yellow Tuberose

BLOOM
May to September

SIZE
Height 8 inches to 5 feet (20 to 150 cm), width to 36 inches (90 cm)

FORM
Broad clump with tall flower stems

HARDINESS
Zone 3, hardy to −40°F (−40°C)

LOCATION
Part shade to full sun

SOIL
Average garden soil, well drained

WATER
Consistently moist, tolerates short drought

PROPAGATION
Division of roots

PLANT PARTNERS
Hollyhock (*Alcea rosea*), Italian Bugloss (*Anchusa bugloss*)

loss of memory. The orange daylily is also the only one capable of colonizing ground with its spreading fleshy rhizomes. One *H. fulva* cousin, *H. esculenta*, was a vegetable eaten fresh or dried and known as *gum tsoy* (golden vegetable) or *gum jum* (gold needles). Equally familiar is the scented spring lemon lily, *H. flava*, which was found in the Levant and came home to England with the Crusaders. It was known as Lily for a Day, with the same one-flower-a-day blooming characteristic as modern daylilies, and also referring to the Greek words *hemera* ("day") and *kallos* ("beauty") from which the plant takes its name. John Hill (*Eden*, 1757) said, "It gilds the Meadows of *Bohemia*; and in *Hungary* perfumes the Air, in some places for many Miles."

Daylilies are so easily grown we presume they don't need good care, but of course they will produce many more flowers if thoughtfully looked after. They favor deep, fertile loam with consistent moisture, but are light eaters. A feeding of manure or bloodmeal in spring as they begin growth is enough for the season, and fertilizers with too much nitrogen will cause them to run to leaf at the expense of flower production. They look after their own deadheading, but removing the seedpods before they swell will keep energy in the plant's crown for better uses. Division is easily accomplished by prising apart the orange roots, but not required frequently. Most daylilies bloom for four to five weeks, and reblooming plants will come back in late summer with a smaller but welcome second flush of flowers.

With thousands of cultivars to choose from, it's almost impossible to make recommendations, with but two exceptions. The intermediate 18-inch (45 cm) 'Happy Returns' is a clear lemon yellow and blooms from June up to frost without a break in flower production. Its low size makes the plant useful for raised beds or bordering a driveway, and it is such a workhorse it's worth having just to count the flowering stems produced in a season. An indispensable choice is 'Hyperion', an old-fashioned scented daylily reaching 4 feet (120 cm) with canary-yellow blossoms and strap-like petals in July and August. It's a good purchase to anchor a daylily collection of one or one hundred, just so long as 'Hyperion' is first.

◄ *The scented lemon lily,* Hemerocallis flava, *is earliest of the daylilies and the basis for many other early hybrids.*

Leopard's Bane
The Daisy Delight

PLANT
Leopard's Bane,
Doronicum cordatum

OTHER NAMES
Caucasian Leopard's Bane

BLOOM
May to June

SIZE
Height 12 to 24 inches (30 to 60 cm), width 12 inches (30 cm)

FORM
Mounding clump

HARDINESS
Zone 4, hardy to –30°F (–34°C)

LOCATION
Light shade to part sun

SOIL
Average garden soil

WATER
Consistent moisture

PROPAGATION
Root division in spring or autumn, seeds

PLANT PARTNERS
Gas Plant (*Dictamnus albus*), Jacob's Ladder (*Polemonium caeruleum*)

It's amazing how leopard's bane keeps its head amid all the controversy. History books fairly leap with arguments over the origins of this pretty spring plant with the sunny yellow daisies. It seems fundamental mistakes may have been made by early Greek and Roman botanists confused about the attributes of two plants, one benign and the other deadly. And it is unfortunate that the name of the deadly variety (the root juices of which were used to poison the spears of Asian leopard hunters) was somehow affixed to the innocuous garden cousin. Suffice to say a debate of great proportion was unleashed by 16th-century herbalists, botanists, and naturalists trying to sort it out, but mostly finger-pointing at the ancients and eating some of the plants to see what would happen. The master botanist John Gerard (*The Herball, or Historie of Plants*, 1597) reports that another fellow (John de Vroede) "did eat verie manie of the rootes at sundrie times, and found them verie pleasant in taste, and verie comfortable." But sadly, the Italian botanist Matthiolus fed them to his dog, and the poor thing died.

But that is all behind us now, for the leopard's bane we know and love is a happy plant of the spring border and no harm to anyone at all. The Latin word *cordatum* ("heart-shaped") describes the smallish serrated leaves that sprout like a fountain from thick roots. It is the earliest of the daisies to bloom, opening semi-double flowers with pure yellow rays surrounding a deeper yellow disk in May and continuing for four to five weeks. For the considerable number of gardeners who dote on the composite form of daisy flowers, leopard's bane is an early joy. It comes at just the right moment to complement May tulips and help hide the ripening foliage of the earlier daffodils. Leopard's bane is also a natural partner to Virginia bluebells (*Mertensia virginiana*), blue forget-me-nots (*Myosotis alpestris*), pansies and violas, and fat clumps of blue scillas.

Leopard's bane is an accommodating plant that asks only to stay out of the hottest sun. It will grow in quite shady areas, but puts on the best show and most flowers in light shade to part sun. Planted in a group of three or five, it will lift a dismal corner of the garden in average soil that may be slightly heavy and, like everything else, grows best with consistent moisture. In too much sun the plants will go dormant at the

In light shade or partial sun, leopard's bane is a reliable friend for four weeks in spring. The species plant is summer dormant, but hybrid 'Madam Mason' can keep its leaves going all season.

beginning of summer, and in part shade the leaves may become a bit tatty and need to be cut back.

Several species and hybrids of *Doronicum* are available in plants and seed, and at varying heights. 'Finesse' has flowers about 3 inches (8 cm) across on 24-inch (60 cm) stems and is a little later to bloom, and 'Magnificum' has larger flowers and is taller, to 30 inches (75 cm). 'Miss Mason' (sometimes 'Mme. Mason') grows about 24 inches (60 cm) high and is very early flowering with many blossoms and charming waved leaves. It will tolerate full sun in the north and can be cut back for a second flush of blooms (apply a little fertilizer if you want a big burst of flowers second time around). 'Spring Beauty' (or 'Frühlingspracht') is earliest of all the doronicums and has double flowers. A larger plant in every respect is the related species *D. plantagineum*, plantain leopard's bane or showy leopard's bane. Its hybrid is 'Harpur Crewe' (sometimes known as 'Excelsum'), which the American plantswoman Judy Glattstein writes is "about the color of New York City taxicabs."

Lily-of-the-Valley
The Return of Happiness

PLANT
Lily-of-the-Valley, *Convallaria majalis*

OTHER NAMES
Lily of the Vale, Our Lady's Tears, Ladder-to-Heaven, Lily Constancy, Mugget

BLOOM
Spring, May to June

SIZE
Height 8 inches (20 cm)

FORM
Spreading, mat-forming

HARDINESS
Zone 3, hardy to −40°F (−40°C)

LOCATION
Part shade to full shade

SOIL
Humusy soil with leaf litter

WATER
Moist in spring, drought-tolerant in summer

PROPAGATION
Divide rhizomes in autumn

PLANT PARTNERS
Snakeshead Fritillary (*Fritillaria meleagris*, hardy tuber), Red Barrenwort (*Epimedium* ✕ *rubrum*)

That shy plant — the lily of the vale,
That loves the ground, and from the sun withholds
Her pensive beauty, from the breeze her sweets.

WILLIAM WORDSWORTH

In the Victorian language of flowers, lily-of-the-valley signifies "the return of happiness," and that is just what one can expect in the month of May when the garden is brimming with new buds and *Convallaria majalis* scents the air. The botanical name derives from *convallis*, "a valley," and *majalis*, "belonging to May." But the ambitious rhizomes of this sentimental favorite have no intention of remaining valley-bound. A lover of deciduous woods, lily-of-the-valley is a good plant for shady corners where nothing else will grow and some ground cover is needed. It is a wild flower of the English countryside, and the herbalist Mrs. M. Greve (*A Modern Herbal*, 1931) recounts that the sweet fragrance of the flowers "draws the nightingale from hedge and bush, and leads him to choose his mate in the recesses of the glade."

Plants with particular beauty or appealing scent collect much local lore, and not all of it pretty. An old Sussex legend recounts that lily-of-the-valley first appeared in St. Leonard's Forest, springing from the blood shed by the saint in combat with the dragons that lurked about that part of the country. And there are, in fact, carpets of the flowers in St. Leonard's Forest today. The image of scented white bells springing from blood-soaked ground is certainly lurid, but not entirely beyond imagination. In more recent times a potent cardiac tonic was prepared from the blossoms and used in World War I to treat gassed soldiers directly on the bloody battlefields. "Golden Water" or *Aqua Aurea* was first distilled from the petals of lily-of-the-valley in the 16th century and was so costly, many brought the wild plants into their gardens for home manufacture. Its use dates back to ancient times, appearing in the fourth-century journal of Apuleius, who claims the plant was received from Apollo. It was an ingredient in love potions, and Robert Louis Stevenson wrote of its uses in the

Lily-of-the-valley grows from "pips," small rhizomes that grow just beneath the surface of the soil. Their foliage begins to brown in August, but a bed shared with ferns will hide the aging leaves.

first chapter of *Kidnapped*, "It is good, ill or well, and whether man or woman…. Likewise for sprains, rub it in; and for the cholic, a greate spoonful in the hour."

The simple charm of lily-of-the-valley has found a place in the hearts of distinguished gardeners. George Schenk, the masterful shade gardener, describes the two blades of foliage as "alert fox-ear leaves" with convex surfaces that slant slightly backwards and deliver rainwater directly down to the roots. Gertrude Jekyll grew "broad sheets of leaf and bloom, from which thousands of flowers can be gathered without making gaps, or showing that any have been removed; when the bloom is over the leaves still stand in handsome masses till they are hidden by the fast-growing bracken." But Vita Sackville-West was perplexed — "They have queer habits; I tried to grow them under trees, which is their natural condition, but they seem to prefer coming up in the middle of a stony path. Plants are really most unpredictable."

Lily-of-the-valley grows from pips that are actually crown buds with a section of rhizome attached. Plant them 2 to 3 inches (5 to 7.5 cm) deep in rich organic soil with leaf mulch over top and some compost or aged manure applied each autumn. The pips will extend their roots horizontally just under the leaf mulch, and once established, pop up sprigs of leaf and flower as they go along. They can colonize an area under deciduous trees very easily if the soil is moist in spring when they make their run for territory. Very old plantings may cease to flower and can be rejuvenated by dividing the mats and spacing them with room to grow. Lily-of-the-valley is a good groundcover in dry shade, but the leaves turn brown in late summer despite any love or moisture you lavish on them. However, Ms. Jekyll found the solution to this predicament by planting them interspersed with ferns to hide the foliage as it ages. A washy pink variety ('Rosea') appears from time to time in the marketplace, and another slow-growing selection with streaked leaves of green and cream ('Striata'). The over-large 'Fortin's Giant' is a shocking thing to encounter in the garden and leaves one wondering if we have all fallen down the rabbit hole with Alice.

Lupine
The Crossing Guard's Flower

Lupines present the largest blossom heads of the late spring season, and their star-like leaves, developing from earliest spring, are a polite reminder of the extravagant flower spikes soon to come. The Egyptians cultivated the ancient white lupine, *Lupinus albus*, an annual plant grown for animal forage and as a green-manure fertilizer for their fields. Lupines are legumes and have the ability to intercept gaseous nitrogen in air and convert it into solid form, depositing the nutrient in the soil, and this works as well in our own gardens as it did for the Egyptians.

The Romans (always interested in cuisine — *tutti a mangiare!*) grew annual lupines for food, and Pliny says, "If taken commonly at meals, it will contribute a fresh color and a cheerful countenance," which is as much to say — a lupine a day keeps the doctor away. In that vein, a rigid lupine diet was inflicted on Protogenus, an artist of repute living in third-century B.C. Rhodes. Lupines were thought to induce flights of creative fancy, and Protogenus ate nothing but lupines and water for seven years (if we can believe that…), while at work on a hunting scene featuring a depiction of a mad dog with frothing mouth. Considerable discussion has gone on since as to whether the frothing dog was meant to represent the artist's madness from a restricted diet. And who could blame him? As is often the pattern, people and events came to their senses in the 18th century when it was noted that lupines were better for cosmetic use than as a comestible and could be used by "ladies to smooth the face, soften the features and make the few charmes they possess a little powerful" (Rev. W. Hanbury, *A Complete Body of Planting and Gardening*, 1770).

The botanical name *Lupinus* is taken from the Greek word *lupe*, meaning "grief," and refers to the extraordinarily bitter seeds of the plant that constricted the taster's face in a grief-like grimace. Indeed, the seeds were said to be bitter and strong enough to kill a hippopotamus outright, and that is something to consider (although we now know they are very toxic). The perennial garden lupine was an elusive species for some time, except for a few like *L. perennis*, the "Virginian Lupine," brought back to Britain from the American colonies in 1637 by the plantsman John Tradescant. It was to everyone's benefit that 250 years later, George Russell of York, England, developed the Russell hybrids, which have been the most colorful garden lupines in contemporary

PLANT
Lupine, *Lupinus* species and hybrids

OTHER NAMES
Wolfsbohne (German)

BLOOM
May to June

SIZE
Height 2 to 4 feet (60 to 120 cm), spread 2 to 3 feet (60 to 90 cm)

FORM
Broad clump with flower spikes

HARDINESS
Zone 4, hardy to −30°F (−34°C)

LOCATION
Full sun

SOIL
Sandy garden soil, well drained

WATER
Consistently moist, tolerates drought after blooming

PROPAGATION
Seeds

PLANT PARTNERS
Lady's Mantle (*Alchemilla mollis*), Rose 'The Fairy' (*Rosa* 'The Fairy')

Lupines are most unlikely flowers; their pea-like florets are so systematically arranged. They are members of the extensive legume family, with the valuable ability to fix nitrogen in the soil and feed themselves.

times. Russell was a retired railroad crossing guard and amateur plant breeder and began his lupine project at age 60, working until he was 75 to achieve success.

Lupines prefer a slightly acid soil and are easy to grow in a well-drained sunny site amended with peat moss. The new 'Band of Nobles' strain reaches a height of 48 inches (120 cm), and dwarf varieties such as 'Minarette' and 'Dwarf Lulu' are half that height. Perennial lupines resent root disturbance and are best started from seeds in pots indoors or simply sown into the open ground and kept moist.

Oriental Poppy
The Parachute Flower

I sing the Poppy! The frail snowy week!
The flower of Mercy! That within its heart
Doth keep "a drop of serene" for human need,
A drowsy balm for every bitter smart.
For happy hours the Rose will idly blow —
The Poppy hath a charm for pain and woe.

MARY A. BARR

Gardeners love a bargain, and oriental poppies are just the ticket, delivering maximum color impact from one or two plants in a small space. They accomplish this by flaunting over-sized crepe-like petals with intensely saturated pigments and standing tall over most everything else in leaf at that time. Their success invites some caustic remarks about brightness and garish colors, but then, excellence always has its detractors. The cranky plantsman Henry Mitchell said oriental poppies "may achieve heights of gaudiness undreamed of outside a flag factory…[there is] an orange red that can be seen as far as there is daylight." No doubt he was thinking of the great scarlet poppy, *Papaver bracteatum*, now considered to be a variety of *P. orientale*, and a genetic contributor to all modern hybrids of any hue.

The poppy takes its name from *popig*, which was an Anglo-Saxon word for "sleep." Classical mythology says Somnus, God of Sleep, created poppies as a sedative for Ceres, who had such fatigue that she was neglecting the corn crop. Ceres drank tea made from the cases of poppy seeds and had a wonderful slumber, awakening to find the crops revived. Depictions of Ceres often show her wearing a garland of corn and field poppies. Allusions to sleep are appropriate, for the opium poppy, *P. somniferum*, has been with us since prehistoric ages. It is an annual plant precursor of the oriental poppy and has been used as a sedative for longer than anyone can say. Although *somniferum* means "sleep bearing," it is well known that the plant provides the base material for the manufacture of opium products such as morphine and heroin. Much legal issue is

PLANT
Oriental Poppy, *Papaver orientale*, *P. bracteatum*

OTHER NAMES
Mawseed

BLOOM
May to June

SIZE
2 to 4 feet (60 to 120 cm)

FORM
Sprawling clumps, flower stems 24 to 36 inches (60 to 90 cm)

HARDINESS
Zone 4, hardy to –30°F (–34°C)

LOCATION
Full sun

SOIL
Organic soil with peat moss and sand, well drained

WATER
Consistent moisture in spring, tolerates short drought

PROPAGATION
Root cuttings in late summer, division in autumn

PLANT PARTNERS
Siberian Iris (*I. sibirica*), Toadflax 'Canon Went' (*Linaria purpurea*)

During daylight, the tissue-thin poppy petals reveal a heart of darkness. When the sun sets, they gently fold over their smudgy stamens.

taken by police agencies with this plant that roams wild over every continent, including many backyards. But it doesn't readily lend itself to cottage industry and is best appreciated as a spectacular, self-seeding flower with double, bomb-type petals. Oriental poppies symbolize "silence" in the Victorian language of flowers, and this may be a reference to the drug-induced slumber of their cousin, *P. somniferum*, for they do not contain the narcotic drug themselves. Gerard's opinion was "Poppie procureth sleepe....It mitigateth all kinds of paines, but it leaveth behind it oftentimes a mischiefe woorse than the disease it selfe....Opium somewhat too plentiful eaten doth also bring death."

Oriental poppies are up and growing early in spring and can be recognized by their fuzzy green leaves reaching for the warm sun. They grow at a fast pace and then send up thick flower stalks with large knobby buds. It's most interesting to watch the buds crack and slowly open over a few days, for the large petals contained inside are as intricately packed and folded as sky parachutes. Planted in bright sun and soil that is moist, well drained, and enriched with aged manure, oriental poppies will bloom for three weeks. Their foliage gradually extends to 24 inches (60 cm) and then lies down to die in July, a messy process that can be hidden by other strategically placed perennials. Gertrude Jekyll used a great cloud of annual white baby's breath (*Gypsophila elegans*) to mask the dying poppy leaves; blue Russian sage (*Perovskia atriplicifolia*) blooms at the same time and works just as well to conceal the gap. Poppies deeply resent root disturbance, but it is possible to take root cuttings in late summer when the plants are dormant, or divide the clump in autumn. But they do best if left undisturbed; it's best to increase your collection with purchased plants.

It doesn't take many oriental poppies to make a statement about color and exuberance in spring. Those who love them (a larger group than those who don't) dot the borders with one or two plants every so often. Some of the old varieties are still available and worth having, like fire engine red 'Beauty of Livermore', crimson and violet 'Waterloo', deep maroon 'Mahony', and 'Darkness'. Wonderful modern cultivars include 'Perry's White', salmon pink 'Queen Alexandra' and 'Helen Elizabeth', deep purple 'Patty's Plum', and soft pink 'Degas'.

Peony
The Plant of Bashful Shame

PLANT
Peony, *Paeonia* hybrids

OTHER NAMES
Chinese Peony

BLOOM
May to June

SIZE
Height 2 1/2 to 4 feet (75 to 120 cm), spread 3 feet (90 cm)

FORM
Broadly spreading clump

HARDINESS
Zone 4, hardy to –30°F (–34°C)

LOCATION
Part shade to full sun

SOIL
Fertile garden soil with aged manure, well drained

WATER
Consistently moist in spring, tolerates short drought

PROPAGATION
Division of roots in early autumn

PLANT PARTNERS
Perennial Geranium 'Johnson's Blue' (*G.* 'Johnson's Blue'), Persian Onion 'Purple Sensation' (*Allium hollandicum* or *A. aflatunense*, hardy bulb)

Everything about the peony is enduring. They last forever, or at least 100 years, which is long enough, and the American gardening author Eleanor Perenyi says, "They are almost immortal, even when hopelessly neglected." Their history is fathomless, buried in the unknowable regions of China, Mongolia, and Siberia. And were it not for intrepid explorers carrying seeds back to European monastery gardens, we wouldn't know them at all.

The plant takes its name from Paeon, an ancient physician and God of Healing, who used the brittle roots to heal an injury given to Pluto by Hercules. Theophrastus described the peony in 320 B.C. (*Enquiry into Plants*) as a plant of supernatural powers. Pliny and Theophrastus warned "that of necessity it must be gathered in the night, for if any man shall pluck of the fruit in the daytime, being seen of the woodpecker, he is in danger to lose his eyes." Furthermore, to remove the peony from the ground, a hungry dog must be tied to a string that is in turn tied to the peony. The dog should be tempted with roasted meat and led to uproot the peony in his scramble to reach the meal. The ears of all present must be stuffed with cotton, for anyone hearing the groan of the plant as it is wrenched from the soil is certain to be struck down permanently. These arrangements require the participation of several persons and a dog, and perhaps are the reason most gardeners are content to leave a peony alone.

Long ago it was thought peonies could be divided into male and female species. The roots of the single-petaled male species were harvested for use in medicinal preparations to treat disorders of the head and nerves. Gerard recommended it to "those that are troubled in the night with the disease called the Nightmare…and they are also good against melancholic dreames." Seeds of the plant were strung into a necklace and worn as a charm against evil spirits or found kitchen use as advised by *Mrs. Glasse's Cookery* (1796) to "stick the cream with Peony kernels." The scented double-petaled species peony presumed to be female was the breeding source for the hybrid plants we know today. Scent has always been a desirable characteristic in the breeding of peonies, and much was done to develop this by the French breeder of lilacs, M. Lemoine. The peony signified "Bashful Shame" in the Victorian language of flowers, and it was thought to be embarrassed because of its "ill odour." This was a reference to certain single and semi-double species peonies that have a curious rank odor to their pollen. But fully double blossoms are often possessed of wonderful sweetness as fine as a rose.

Many peonies outlast the gardeners who plant them, and getting them properly settled into their holes will ensure flowers for life. They need well-drained fertile soil enriched with aged manure, and a consistent amount of moisture, all delivered to a sunny place in the garden. The most important point is to plant peonies shallowly, with the top of the crown covered with just an inch (2.5 cm) of soil. Plants set too low in the hole will refuse to bloom, perhaps requiring removal and the services of a strong dog. If brave souls are intent on dividing the brittle roots of a peony, do it in late summer and aim for four or five pink buds on each division. The earliest peony to bloom is *P. tenuifolia* 'Plena', the scented and double scarlet fern leaf peony, opening in May. By selecting early, mid-season, and late-blooming varieties, the flowering period can be stretched to six weeks. Most double peonies have some scent, particularly those developed in France by M. Lemoine. Plants to covet for their sweet perfume include 'Festiva Maxima' and 'Festiva Supreme', both double whites flecked with red at the center, deepest maroon-red 'Karl Rosenfeld', the huge chrysanthemum-like bombs of silvery pink 'Mons. Jules Elie', and the apple-blossom pink 'Sarah Bernhardt'.

'Mandarin Red' Japanese tree peonies (Paeonia suffruticosa) *make massive blooms on small woody shrubs. Turid Forsyth uses the scented petals in aromatic dried potpourris.*

Perennial Cornflower
In Bachelor Pockets

PLANT
Perennial Cornflower, *Centaurea montana*

OTHER NAMES
Mountain Bluet, Bachelor Button

BLOOM
May to July

SIZE
Height 24 inches (60 cm), spread 24 inches (60 cm)

FORM
Spreading clump

HARDINESS
Zone 4, hardy to –30°F (–34°C)

LOCATION
Part shade to full sun

SOIL
Average garden soil, well drained

WATER
Moist to slightly dry, will not tolerate wet feet

PROPAGATION
Root division in spring or autumn, summer cuttings, seeds

PLANT PARTNERS
Dames Rocket (*Hesperis matronalis*), Catmint 'Six Hills Giant' (*Nepeta* hybrid)

What could be more genuinely our own than the image of blue cornflowers roaming the meadows and rows of farmland? Wrong. The sparkly blue flowers were roaming Britain during the late glacial period, long before our ancestors found reason to depart those shores with seeds in their pockets. Nevertheless, cornflowers have found their way into our sense of place. The annual blue-bottle cornflower (*C. cyanus*) was first to "pester the corn fields," blunting the reaping hooks so badly that it was also called hurt-sickle. It was a cultivated garden plant from Tudor times, along with the musk-scented sweet sultan or sultan's flower (*C. moschata*).

The botanical name *Centaurea* is from the Greek word *kentaur*, "a centaur" (half man, half horse), and refers to the legend of Chiron the Centaur, who was accidentally wounded by a poison arrow thrown by Jupiter. Chiron suffered terribly but found a cure in the cornflower. Possibly the curative cornflower was greater knapweed (*C. scabiosa*), which for centuries was a natural folk remedy for wounds and the pestilence. The rich crimson flowers grow wild in pastures, borders of fields, and roadsides throughout Britain, and the plant was a key ingredient in the 14th-century ointment Save and was also used with pepper for loss of appetite.

The perennial cornflower (*C. montana*) familiar to gardeners in North America was introduced from the Pyrenees before 1596, but was little appreciated at the time. And that may be why so many unmarried young men departing for the New World carried it away with them, and much to our benefit. Perennial cornflower blooms for about four weeks and then can be cut back almost to the ground. New growth will regenerate with the possibility of additional flower production if there is sufficient sunlight. The plant will adapt to light shade, but in more sun and rich, soft soil it will spread to make a good groundcover and possibly make some seedlings. Consistent moisture encourages strong growth, but *C. montana* resents wet feet and should always have adequate drainage. The violet-blue ray florets of the species have an electric brightness that shines in the garden and is every bit as beautiful as the hybrid colors. A clear blue flower is produced by 'Caerulea', and 'Grandiflora' is a larger light-blue blossom. 'Rosea' is pink, 'Alba' is white, and 'Violetta' is darker violet than the species.

Cornflowers are among the oldest of cultivated cottage garden flowers. Both annual and perennial plants have been grown for hundreds of years, and in many colors. The electric blue perennial cornflower is largest, with 3-inch (7.5 cm) blooms. The sweet sultan (Centaurea moschata) *annual cornflower is smallest, and also scented.*

Perennial Geranium
The Gardens of Our Enemies

PLANT
Perennial Geranium, *Geranium macrorrhizum, G. sanguineum, G. 'Claridge Druce,' G. robertianum*

OTHER NAMES
Cranesbill, Storksbill, Alum Root, Dove's Foot, Old Maid's Nightcap, Shameface

BLOOM
May to August

SIZE
Height 12 inches (30 cm), spreading width to 24 inches (60 cm)

FORM
Mounding clumps

HARDINESS
Zone 4, hardy to –30°F (–34°C)

LOCATION
Light shade to full sun

SOIL
Well-drained organic, woodland soil

WATER
Consistent moisture, will tolerate short drought

PROPAGATION
Root division, tip cuttings, seed

PLANT PARTNERS
Spotted Dead Nettle (*Lamium maculatum*), Big Betony (*Stachys grandiflora*)

Little Herb Robert,
Bright and small,
Peeps from the bank
Or the old stone wall.

Little Herb Robert,
His leaf turns red;
He's wild geranium,
So it is said.

CICELY MARY BARKER

There is an army of silent plants marching through our gardens at every moment, but perhaps that isn't news. We are seemingly frozen in a crisis of choice, for perennial geraniums are a limitless family of friendly and enticing plants with intentions of colonizing the corners of the world in a graceful and useful manner — never giving offense, always finding a purpose. They are adaptive to every situation and light quality, most soils, and certainly every discerning eye. Which raises the question, how shall we harness this enterprising energy?

The many geranium species are often called cranesbill or storksbill geraniums, referring to the long beaky seed capsules. A good strategy is to select plants that make the most useful groundcovers in sun and shade, and with flowers for the longest period of time. For dry shade sites under trees and on the north side of a fence, nothing gives better and quicker coverage than *Geranium macrorrhizum*, the bigroot geranium, which is eager to spread out its rounded and palmately lobed leaves in mats 8 to 12 inches (20 to 30 cm) high. It was cultivated in the Oxford Botanic Garden in 1658 and is the species with the pungent, citrusy scent from which geranium oil is extracted. The simple five-petaled rosy flowers have prominent stamens which give a fancy effect above the foliage. 'Ingwersen's Variety' is a soft rose shade, and there is an elusive white species sometimes to be found.

Small areas of bright light are happily filled with *G. sanguineum*, the bloody geranium, although blood of such a magenta shade is beyond the ken of modern hematology. The plant makes a tumble of wiry stems and ferny foliage 6 to 12 inches (15 to 30 cm) high and twice as wide for the front of the border or corners of walkways, and there is a dwarf variety ('Shepherd's Warning') only 4 to 6 inches (10 to 15 cm) in stature and good for small patches between rocks. The shade gardener George Schenk has no affinity for this vibrant color and says it "should be planted only in the garden of one's enemy, by secretly shooting the seeds forth with a slingshot or blowpipe." But then he is accustomed to lower light and prefers the less alarming white variety, *G. sanguineum* 'Album', flowering from May to September.

'Johnson's Blue' geranium foliage can be cut back hard after the flowers are finished, and fresh leaves will make an attractive mound until frost.

For open spaces in bright light, *Geranium × oxonianum* 'Claridge Druce' is a successful groundcover, but how a plant or person could be given such a name is hard to understand. However, the appellation seems not to have held it back and the tall 18-inch (45 cm) clumps of shining foliage produce rosy pink funnel-shaped flowers for six to eight weeks in summer. This is a vigorous, free-flowering geranium that seeds itself around, often very conveniently so, and is easy to remove where not wanted. The smart strategy is to collect seedlings and move them to areas in need of groundcover where they efficiently cover the soil and suppress weed growth.

Wild shady places are much benefited by the presence of *G. robertianum*, or herb Robert, and this charming little plant may already be there. Its delicate roots barely skim the surface of the soil as it moves about in dry shade under the tree canopy of forests and dells. The 6-inch (15 cm) delicate ferny foliage has a pungent scent, turning blazing red in autumn, and the small pink flowers bear resemblance to their larger and more evolved cousins. Herb Robert is a wild plant that cannot be confined, but makes a lovely carpet over the soil when allowed to ramble at will. Anyone who thinks this plant is a weed is in desperate need of education.

Siberian Iris
The Good News Messenger

PLANT
Siberian Iris, *Iris siberica*

OTHER NAMES
Fleur de Luce, Flag

BLOOM
May to June

SIZE
24 to 48 inches (60 to 120 cm)

FORM
Thick, mat-forming clump

HARDINESS
Zone 3, hardy to –40°F (–40°C)

LOCATION
Full sun

SOIL
Rich garden soil with added peat
moss and manure

WATER
Consistently moist, will not tolerate
drought

PROPAGATION
Root division in late summer

PLANT PARTNERS
Sundrops (*Oenothera tetragona*),
Rose Campion (*Lychnis coronaria*)

Thou art the Iris, fair among the fairest,
  Who, armed with golden rod
And winged with the celestial azure,
  Bearest the message of some God.

HENRY WADSWORTH LONGFELLOW

There is every opportunity to misunderstand the iris family, for the members are diverse in their origins, dispositions, and preferred growing conditions. About 1600, Gerard catalogued thirteen kinds of rhizomatous irises and three bulbous ones. Fifty years later, Parkinson counted thirty "Flaggs," plus seven English varieties, and thirty Spanish kinds. In the mid-18th century John Hill (author of *The British Herbal*) remarked, "The iris's…appear a confus'd tho' elegant Family. The Species in Nature are many, the Varieties raised by Art are more; and 'tis not in the Common Eye to distinguish which has the certain, which but the casual Distinction." Well, the man hit it right on the head. Today there are more than 200 species from dry, wet, hot, and cold places, and thousands of hybrid cultivars to choose from. And some are very strange, indeed, such as *Iris foetidissima*, which is also known as roast beef plant and has the scent of roasted meat, or something nearly like it. Now what to make of that?

The plant is named after Iris, the messenger of Juno and Goddess of Rainbows. She used her rainbow as a bridge between heaven and earth, carrying messages of only good news, and it was thought the colors in the sky were reflected in the petals of iris blossoms. The ancient Egyptians believed the three falls, or downward-hanging petals, represented the divine qualities of faith, wisdom, and valor, and the entire plant symbolized eloquence. They carved an iris on the forehead of their sphinx so he would be profound in his thoughts.

The Greeks and Romans took a commercial interest in the rhizomes of *Iris germanica*, *I. pallida*, and *I. florentina*, which in dried form is orrisroot, the violet-scented component of the many perfumes and toiletries they manufactured. Even into the 20th century, huge quantities of orrisroot, as much as a million kilograms from one plantation, were harvested in Tuscany, where they were locally known as *giaggiolo*. In the sixth century the Frankish king Clovis replaced the three toads on his banner with three irises, a wise move to avoid historical recognition as the Toad King. Eventually these symbols became the heraldic emblem of the kings of France. The iris was referred to as *Fleur de Luce* and then *Fleur de Lys*, which is the symbol on the French flag today (and not toads).

Siberian irises are the most cold hardy of their tribe, and without the problems that can plague the more statuesque and flamboyant iris categories. Despite their descriptive name, the Siberians are native to northern Europe and were grown in England prior to 1597. They are bright and charming flowers, distinguished from most other

Siberian iris 'Atoll' grows thick with blossoming stems because it gets generous moisture in a sunny position. The thin lance-like leaves make good vertical lines in the summer border and the seedpods are attractive for dried winter arrangements.

irises by their hollow stem, and with reed-like foliage that makes a good vertical reference in the border all season. Siberian irises will bloom for three to four weeks if properly situated. They require full sun, fertile soil enriched with aged manure and peat moss, and consistent moisture with good drainage. Unlike their tall and bearded cousins, which are inclined to topple, Siberian irises stand straight up and carry their perfectly formed flowers like flocks of butterflies hovering over the pointy leaf tips. Siberian iris is often mistaken for a shade-tolerant plant, which it is not. In shady conditions with dry soil, they are quick to sulk and make themselves unhappy. But in bright sunlight and moist soil, they are like an explosion of purple, blue, violet, yellow, and white. There are many hybrids, and among the most distinctive are velvety blue-black 'Caesar's Brother', medium azure 'Perry's Blue', and yellow and white bi-color 'Butter and Sugar'. When older clumps begin to die out in the middle they should be divided with a sharp spade, making several smaller plants.

Solomon's Seal
The Seal of Foreign Relations

PLANT
Solomon's Seal, *Polygonatum biflorum, P. commutatum*

OTHER NAMES
Giant Solomon's Seal, Great Solomon's Seal, True Solomon's Seal, David's Harp, Ladder to Heaven

BLOOM
May to June

SIZE
Height 24 to 48 inches (60 to 120 cm), width 24 inches (60 cm)

FORM
Arching stems

HARDINESS
Zone 4, hardy to –30°F (–34°C)

LOCATION
Shade to part sun

SOIL
Woodland, organic, well drained

WATER
Moist in spring, will tolerate drier weather thereafter

PROPAGATION
Root division

PLANT PARTNERS
Shooting Star (*Dodecatheon meadia*), Forget-Me-Not (*Myosotis alpestris*)

The legend of King Solomon's seal haunts this most graceful woodland plant, native to Northern Europe and Siberia as well as the moist forests of North America. The simple beauty of the plant with such chaste and naive flowers suggests a special symbolism, perhaps lost in time. Each thick underground tuber sends up one perfectly arched shoot with sweetly scented, pendulous waxy-white florets tipped in pale green. Nineteenth-century florists were clever to recognize its elegance and forced the stems for cut-flower sales. The middle European countries were more practical, cutting the new 6- to 8-inch (15 to 20 cm) shoots and preparing them in the manner of asparagus.

The botanical name derives from *poly* ("many") and *gonu* ("knee-joints"), descriptive of the knobby tubers. All the great herbalists were enthusiastic about the properties of Solomon's seal, and it was long associated with healing wounds, clearing skin imperfections, and mending broken bones. A decoction of the tubers was commonly used to treat bruising, and John Gerard (*Catalogue of Plants*, 1596) said it "taketh away in one night or two at most, any bruse, blacke or blew spots gotten by fals or women's wilfulness, in stumbling upon their hastie husband's fists, or such like." Well, one wonders about that. But in a more positive reference, John Parkinson (*Theatrum Botanicum*, 1640) remarked, "The Italian dames, however, doe much use the distilled water of the whole plant of Solomon's Seal for their complexions."

But what to make of the legend of King Solomon and the seal he wore as a signet ring on his right hand? The contemporary interpretation is that the 10th-century B.C. King of the Israelites was knowledgeable in medicinal plants and placed his approval upon *Polygonatum* for its healing powers. However, a perusal of the man's life points in another direction, for Solomon was above all a sensualist and a romantic. He was a lover of women, fine living, and philosophical debate, and received many foreign delegations in his palace. Affairs of state also included affairs of the heart. The adolescent Makeda (Hatshepsut), virgin Queen of Sheba (now Yemen), traveled 1,400 miles (2240 km) on camelback ostensibly to forge new trade agreements between the two nations, but more so drawn by reports of Solomon's practical wisdom and masculine allure. Makeda was precociously intelligent and craved the companionship of

The pugilist's friend, Solomon's seal has been said "to cure a black eye sooner than anything." But for calmer gardeners it will be a strong architectural presence in shady areas all summer.

a like mind and the stimulation of a powerful monarch. She stayed six months with Solomon as he tutored her in statesmanship, and inevitably, their extended negotiations produced a child who became the first king of Ethiopia. It is unclear who seduced whom, but in Solomon's poetic *Song of Songs* are the revealing words, "Set me as a seal upon thy heart…" (*Solomon's Song*, 8.6). And so it could be construed that the lovely dangling florets are Solomon's seals on Makeda's heart.

Solomon's seal is a close relative of the lily-of-the-valley, of which the resemblance is immediately apparent. As a woodland plant, it performs well in shade under trees or in part-sun locations that are moist in spring, and it will tolerate drier conditions in summer. It blooms for four weeks starting in early May, and the arching stems of the plant remain attractive for the entire season. The thick tubers are planted 6 inches (15 cm) deep and can be easily divided in autumn or early spring, and replanted divisions quickly make new clumps. Tubers that have been damaged or cut will still succeed if planted. Occasionally dark seeds are produced and these germinate if sown when fresh and the soft seed coat removed. Solomon's seal is a favorite plant of early spring bumblebees; they struggle to fit into the pendant blossoms and dangle perilously, all for the sake of the sweet nectar contained within.

Yellow Corydalis
The Purifying Flower

PLANT
Yellow Corydalis, *Corydalis lutea*

OTHER NAMES
Yellow Fumitory

BLOOM
May to October

SIZE
Height 12 to 16 inches (30 to 40 cm), width 12 to 24 inches (30 to 60 cm)

FORM
Spreading clump

HARDINESS
Zone 5, hardy to −20°F (−29°C)

LOCATION
Light shade to full sun

SOIL
Slightly alkaline, gravelly, well drained

WATER
Consistently moist, will tolerate some drought

PROPAGATION
Root division in spring, seeds in mid-summer

PLANT PARTNERS
Yellow Archangel (*Lamium galeobdolon*), Bigflower Selfheal (*Prunella grandiflora*)

There is something to be said for a plant that is happy all the time, like the little yellow corydalis (*Corydalis lutea*) that flits about the garden from spring to frost. With nothing better to do than look fetching in odd corners and bloom for the better part of six months, it is sometimes an annual, sometimes a perennial, but always reliably sows itself for a good display next year. Corydalis is part of the larger family of fumitories, all with similar leaves and flowers ranging from yellow and white to pinkish-violet and China blue. Its name is taken from the Greek word *korydalis*, "a crested lark," and is meant to describe the flower heads hovering over the ferny blue-green foliage.

Corydalis lutea is an unpretentious plant of naive demeanor, masking a turbulent past and some interesting cousins. It originated on the Barbary Coast of Northern Africa, where successive conquerors (the Romans, Vandals, Arabs, Turks, Spaniards, French, and Italians) each packed up pots of yellow flowers to take home like floral table arrangements from a wedding. Geoffrey Chaucer wrote about a related species, *Fumaria officinalis*, that was already known on the European continent as Earth Smoke. Exorcists in the Dark Ages made use of the plant for cleansing rituals at St. Gall, the seventh-century Benedictine abbey in Switzerland, where the plants were burned on elaborate geometric garden beds (forerunners of the French *parterre* style) to expel evil spirits from the soil. There was a legend that fumitories of all kinds were not produced from seeds, but from vapors arising out of the earth, likely based on the wispy character of their emerging spring foliage. The idea of cleansing powers was carried forward to the 17th century when fumitories were used to remove freckles and treat leprosy, and an old recipe says the plant is "a most singular thing against hypochondriack melancholy in any person whatsoever."

Yellow corydalis is willing to grow wherever the soil is well drained and slightly alkaline, and it's not unusual to find them popping up in gravel driveways. Their ability to persist in shade, in dryish soil, and among rocks makes them a good choice for planting into soil pockets in rock walls. One 18th-century garden authority (Philip Miller, *The Gardener's Dictionary*) said *C. lutea* "will grow on mortar and is therefore a very proper Plant to grow in Rockwork, or upon old Walls or Buildings, to hide their Deformity." One small plant will seed itself about, guaranteeing progeny for years to

The yellow corydalis is a wonderful plant for a rockery or between large boulders, where it will bloom from May to frost. The ferny blue-green foliage is well suited to softening hard surfaces. Given its own way, yellow corydalis loves to find a perch in stone retaining walls.

come, and its spontaneous presence is appreciated almost anywhere. If it lands where not wanted, a stern look or one swipe of the hand is enough to send it packing. Another cousin worth having is the white fumitory, *C. ochroleuca*, and despite the cumbersome name, its white flowers tipped with yellow are like lace across the garden. Divide corydalis in early spring, or sprinkle seeds on bare soil in midsummer for flowers the following year. The larger cousins, *C. flexuosa* 'Blue Panda' and 'China Blue', are very beautiful, but require slightly acid soil and abundant moisture, and have a shorter blooming period.

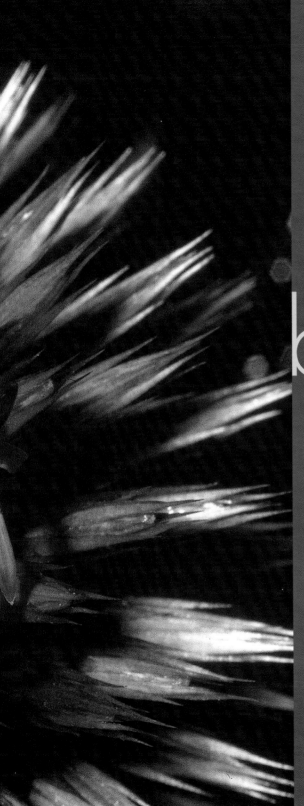

4

MID-SEASON
blooms

"To work in the garden is to be brought into contact with the elements of botany, geography, ecology, genetics, chemistry and entomology — not to mention ornithology, bacteriology and meteorology.... Add to this the infinite number of plants...and it is apparent that no lifetime is long enough in which to explore the resources of a few square yards of ground."

ALICE M. COATS, FLOWERS AND THEIR HISTORIES

Astilbe
Père David's Keepsake

PLANT
Astilbe, *Astilbe × arendsii*,
A. chinensis

OTHER NAMES
False spirea

BLOOM
July to August

SIZE
Height 12 to 36 inches (30 to
90 cm), spread 12 to 24 inches
(30 to 60 cm)

FORM
Thick clump with flower spikes

HARDINESS
Zone 4, hardy to –30°F (–34°C)

LOCATION
Part shade to full sun

SOIL
Rich and organic garden soil, well
drained

WATER
Moist in part shade, wet in full sun,
won't tolerate drought

PROPAGATION
Root division in spring or early
autumn

PLANT PARTNERS
Painted Daisy (*Chrysanthemum
coccineum*), Meadow Rue
(*Thalictrum aquilegifolium*)

Astilbe is such a serviceable plant, and were it better known we would all have more of it. But how long does it take to know the little ways and means of a plant? One would think at least a few hundred years, considering that many of our familiar garden perennials have been in cultivation since the Middle Ages, and we have finally understood what they need and how to use them. But astilbe is fresh from Asia, having been buried in China for longer than anyone can say, and arrived in the west without pedigree in about 1870.

We have not always had the convenience of garden centers in our midst, to acquire plants from great distances and bring them conveniently into our neighborhood. Even into the last century, intrepid botanists and horticulturists have trekked into unknown foreign parts in search of new plants and brought them back, often at great personal peril. Among them was Père Armand David (1826–1900), a French Catholic missionary priest who also happened to be a zoologist with a fondness for plants. After being ordained in 1862, he was sent to Peking to begin a collection of material for the Jardin des Plantes in Paris, a natural history museum funded by the French government. Père David was amazingly successful in collecting 63 animals unknown to western zoologists; 65 birds that had never been described before; 52 new species of rhododendron and an even greater number of unknown gentian species; and his namesake plants, the butterfly bush (*Buddleia davidii*) and the handkerchief tree (*Davidia involucrata*). And in the bottom of his bag, a small personal keepsake — the astilbe.

The new plant was named with the Greek words *a*, "without," and *stilbe*, "brilliance," for truth be known, it was a bit lackluster. Fortune would have it that George Arends, a plant breeder in Ronsdorf, Germany, took an interest in its development and endowed astilbe with the pastel and jewel tones we know today in *Astilbe × arendsii* and the Ronsdorf hybrids. Looking carefully, we see an astilbe or two in almost every garden, although they often seem uncertainly placed or in isolation by the garage. These are indicators of misinformation or an absence of any information at all. Astilbe is capable of making a bright display and imparting much style to the landscape all season, if only we can understand the context it requires. Unfortunately, it is often sold as a shade plant, implying that it is happy to struggle in dry shade and hard clay soil, advice that is entirely wrong.

Astilbe wants highly organic soil, bright light, and constant moisture. It is probably a plant of moist riverbanks in open meadows of China (although we won't ever have the full story on that). Astilbe will grow in part shade with moist soil and produce an acceptable number of flower stalks. But it makes many more flower stalks and a firecracker display of color in full sun if the soil is decidedly wet (but not boggy, for it must have drainage) and if it has a shredded leaf or shredded bark mulch to keep the moisture from evaporating. These bright and wet circumstances also favor an attractive display of handsome foliage all season, and if the flower stalks are left standing, they are ornamental in winter snow.

Astilbe has the most impact when planted in a group of five or more and it is ideal for groundcover purposes, for with enough moisture it forms dense clumps that will mesh together and fill an area. Although astilbes of any size are useful for groundcover, *A. chinensis* 'Pumila' is a charming and effective dwarf variety that spreads readily, forming a dense mat of sharply incised leaves; it bears many 12-inch (30 cm) panicles of deep magenta pink or pale mauve flowers in late summer. Taller astilbes with intense color include white 'Avalanche' and 'Deutschland', dark red 'Etna' and bright red 'Bremen', rich pink 'Bressingham Beauty' and light pink 'Europa'. The deep red stems of the red cultivars are an added feature, and astilbes can bloom in the garden for six weeks if early, mid-season, and late-blooming varieties are combined.

To lengthen the flowering period of hybrid astilbes like 'William Reeves', keep the soil moist or wet and provide organic mulch to prevent moisture evaporation.

Two astilbes with enough size and ornamental characteristics to be grown as single specimens are 'Superba' and 'Ostrich Plume'. *Astilbe taquetii* 'Superba' stands almost 4 feet (120 cm) tall, with large compound leaves and double-toothed leaflets, and erect panicles of vivid magenta pink flowers carried high above the foliage on strong stems. It blooms in late summer and has more heat tolerance than other *arendsii* hybrids. Perhaps most curious is *A.* × *arendsii* 'Ostrich Plume', a beautiful 3-foot (90 cm) plant with arching open sprays of coral-pink flowers that drape in a semi-cascade fashion in mid-season. It bears mentioning that astilbe is sometimes erroneously known by the common name of false spirea. In fact, there is a deciduous shrub (*Sorbaria sorbifolia*) known commonly as false spirea and its leaves bear some resemblance to those of astilbe, but they are not the same plant and have no other shared features. However, this bit of misinformation may take another century or two to straighten out.

Baby's Breath
The Garden's Mask

PLANT
Baby's Breath, *Gypsophila paniculata*

OTHER NAMES
Chalk Plant

BLOOM
June to August

SIZE
Height 2 to 3 feet (60 to 90 cm), width 3 feet (90 cm)

FORM
Sprawling clump

HARDINESS
Zone 4, hardy to –30°F (–34°C)

LOCATION
Full sun

SOIL
Light, well drained, alkaline

WATER
Consistently moist

PROPAGATION
Seed, stem cuttings

PLANT PARTNERS
Perennial Flax (*Linum perenne*), Coral Bells (*Heuchera sanguinea*)

Gertrude Jekyll described *Gypsophila paniculata* as a mist in the garden's early light, but despite that ethereal vision, baby's breath makes a strong point about what it likes. The name is taken from the Greek words *gypsos* ("gypsum") and *philos* ("loving") to make the point that it must have light, well-draining, humusy, alkaline soil with pH between 7.0 and 7.8 — not to put too fine a point on it. That information rather takes the romance away from the misty moment, but there you have the reality of plant life. If alkaline soil isn't available, the planting hole can be amended with a handful of lime or wood ash to reach the comfortably alkaline level.

If ever there was a plant to heal, mend, and mask the rough spaces in a garden bed, baby's breath is the best candidate. It puts up a frothing mass of wiry fish-line stems massed with 1/4-inch (5 mm) double blooms of sparkling white and feathery texture, and keeps up the display for six weeks. Gertrude Jekyll put it between all her poppy clumps to mask the dying foliage and fill their gaps, and it also works well to lighten the atmosphere around the ponderous leaves of hollyhocks and the stiff darkness of an evergreen yew hedge. 'Bristol Fairy' baby's breath is a traditional white choice and also has a pink counterpart, 'Pink Fairy'. The pink category has been further developed to include *G.p.* 'Flamingo', a cultivar name that makes bells go off for it has large mauve-pink blossoms, and also 'Rosy Veil', a clear pink. Perhaps these ethereal beauties are becoming a bit too worldly?

Baby's breath may burn out in late summer, when it should be sheared back and given a bit of liquid fertilizer to stimulate a second bloom in September lasting into the frosty first days of October. The low-growing species is *G.p. repens*, creeping baby's breath, in white or pink ('Bodgeri'), which reaches 12 inches (30 cm) in height and will spread out as a groundcover. It should be used more often and can make a glorious hazy cloud spilling out over massive stone walls in a raised bed. Annual baby's breath, *Gypsophila elegans*, is easily grown from seed and is available in white ('Covent Garden' and 'White Giant'), rose, and a shocking purple, all good for containers in summer, and for cutting to dry for winter arrangements. Stagger two plantings of the annual baby's breath six weeks apart for a season of continuous bloom.

Against a battalion of lilies in bud, a cloud of Baby's Breath fills the gaps between perennial clumps. When the flowers fall, cut it back and feed generously with manure to stimulate a second bloom in September.

Bee Balm
The Gift of Tea

PLANT
Bee Balm, *Monarda didyma*

OTHER NAMES
Oswego Tea, Bergamot, Scarlet Bee
Balm

BLOOM
July to August

SIZE
Height 30 to 36 inches (75 to
90 cm), spread 12 inches (30 cm)

FORM
Spreading clump

HARDINESS
Zone 4, hardy to –30°F (–34°C)

LOCATION
Part shade to full sun

SOIL
Average garden soil, well drained

WATER
Consistently moist, tolerates short
drought

PROPAGATION
Root division

PLANT PARTNERS
Delphinium 'Connecticut Yankee'
(*Delphinium* hybrids), Daylily
(*Hemerocallis*)

We are so delighted when an admired plant originates on our own shores, in view of our brief hold on the continent. Bee balm (*Monarda didyma*) and its several species are indigenous to North America and were among the plants John Tradescant "the younger" (that is, not his father John the Elder, who was an intrepid botanizer and gardener to Charles I) brought back from a collecting expedition to the Virginia Colony in 1637. It was a plant of compelling interest, particularly for its delicious scent as well as the fancy red blossoms. Parkinson described it in his *Theatrum Botanicum* just a short 36 months later as *Origanum fistulosum*, a wild mint of America, obviously twigging to the four-sided stem, characteristic of all mint family brethren.

It required a gift of fresh seed in 1744 from the American botanist John Bartram to bring monarda to attention again. Bartram had found Native Americans in Oswego, New York, on the banks of Lake Ontario, brewing tea from the leaves of wild bee balm (*M. fistula*). In England there was agreement that the plant was satisfactory for tea purposes, as well as flavoring the alcoholic beverages hock and Moselle cup, although nothing much was done about that, and the plant continued to be grown as a garden ornamental.

It is an interesting coincidence that the Chinese made a gift of tea to a popular British prime minister, Charles, the second Earl Grey, in about 1830. Earl Grey was a progressive legislator, responsible for the act abolishing the African slave trade in Britain and a founding member of the reform group, Friends of the People, which lobbied for more equal representation and parliamentary reform. The Chinese tea was expressly for the use of the Imperial household and was brought to Earl Grey by a British envoy who had saved the life of a mandarin. It was a uniquely scented black tea, the secret ingredient of which was oil of the bergamot orange, an orange-lemon hybrid named after the town of Bergamo in northern Italy. The oranges yield exceptionally rich aromatic oil that was used in perfumery as early as 1688. And wouldn't you know, the bergamot tea had quite the same scent as American bee balm growing in many English gardens. It didn't take long for assumptions to be made about the similar scents, and thereafter bee balm was also referred to as bergamot. Earl Grey was particularly fond of the tea and gave the recipe to his tea merchant, Twinings. And the rest is history.

Monarda didyma is called bee balm because of the affection bees show for the blossoms, which produce generous amounts of sweet nectar. It grows in most garden soils except heavy clay and will provide four to six weeks of bloom in half a day of light. The stems stand 30 to 36 inches (75 to 90 cm) tall, and the blossoms carry a crown of nectar-bearing tubular coronets around the head which hummingbirds relish. Many cultivars are red, but other colors are soft pink 'Croftway Pink', pale lavender 'Beauty of Cobham', and violet-purple 'Blue Stocking'. Bee balm occasionally has mildew after excessively humid weather, but this does not injure the plants. Mildew-resistant varieties are 'Purple Mildew Resistant', 'Gardenview Scarlet', and clear pink 'Marshall's Delight'. Keeping the plants well watered will help to prevent stress-induced mildew. Bee balm spreads from shallow roots and can be easily divided. Removing roots from the outside of the clump when necessary will keep it in one place.

The prominently placed nectaries of bee balm are a magnet for hummingbirds as they get ready for their flight south. Bee balm sprouts a secondary bloom right up through the center of the flower.

Coral Bells
Fairies Wanted, Please Apply

PLANT
Coral Bells, *Heuchera sanguinea*,
H. americana

OTHER NAMES
Alum Root

BLOOM
June to August

SIZE
Height 12 to 18 inches (30 to
45 cm), width 12 inches (30 cm)

FORM
Small clump with erect flower stems

HARDINESS
Zone 4, hardy to –30°F (–34°C)

LOCATION
Partial shade

SOIL
Organic woodland soil, well drained

WATER
Consistently moist, does not tolerate
drought

PROPAGATION
Division, seed, stem and leaf cuttings

PLANT PARTNERS
Lady's Mantle (*Alchemilla mollis*),
Carpathian Harebell (*Campanula
carpatica*)

We just know that *Heuchera sanguinea*, with its rippled leaves and swaying stems of colorful little bells, would inspire all sorts of folklore in Europe. But here in North America we have a different kind of imagination, if any at all, and no fairies or wee people are associated with coral bells. It's a pity, for this seems a lost opportunity for a bit of our own mythology. Coral bells is a plant of dry woods and shady wildflower gardens, just the sorts of places in which wee folk should be up to their tricks — think of the venue for mischief with 70 species of heuchera native to Mexico and Arizona. The neat basal rosettes send up thin 18-inch (45 cm) stems that nearly can't be seen, leaving the white, pink, or red bell flowers suspended above the foliage in a fetching manner.

Heuchera is a fine edging plant for garden pathways or for massing to cover a broad corner. It grows best in moist and organic soil with good drainage, and as with so many perennials, blooming can be extended by removing the spent flower stems. Coral bells will accept a full sun location if the soil is moist and watering is consistent, for the intense ultraviolet light is scorching on its tender leaves. Hummingbirds are especially fond of the little flowers, and particularly coral-red 'Matin Bells', deep scarlet 'Fire Bird', cherry red 'Pluie de Feu (Rain of Fire)', and deep red 'Scarlet Sentinel'. Red 'Scintillation' and white 'Green Ivory' are taller plants with 24- to 30-inch (60 to 75 cm) flower scapes.

Plant breeders are (this time) on the side of the angels for their work in developing *Heuchera americana*, American alumroot, which has formed the genetic basis for the many coral bells with dark bronze, chocolate brown, and plumy purple leaves, some suffused with pewter flushes and patterns. These cultivars are grown for the deep colors of their ornamental foliage, and their creamy urn-shaped flowers are a secondary feature. The first of many dark-leaved heucheras was 'Palace Purple', which proved to be a variable plant from seed, but has the pleasant habit of seeding itself around. All the dark cultivars emerge in spring with an intense luster to the leaves that gradually deepens as the foliage expands. Covering the woody stems with fresh soil and encouraging them to root can delay the need to divide mature plants. Coral bells has a long life in the garden and should be divided after three or four years; when you divide, discard the oldest woody stems and replant the younger sections.

'Palace Purple' was the first dark-leaved coral bell with creamy little bells on wiry stems. The leaves are first dark purple-bronze, and then turn to bronzy green with a deep purple reverse side. The new hybrids are deeply purple with pewter markings.

Foxglove
The Silent Fox

PLANT
Foxglove, *Digitalis purpurea*,
D. grandiflora, D. ferruginea

OTHER NAMES
Finger Flower, Fairy Glove, Purple
Foxglove

BLOOM
June to July and August

SIZE
Height 2 to 5 feet (60 to 150 cm)

FORM
Basal rosette with central flower
spike

HARDINESS
Zone 5, hardy to –20°F (–29°C)

LOCATION
Light shade to full sun

SOIL
Woodland soil, organic, fertile

WATER
Consistent moisture, will not
tolerate drought

PROPAGATION
Seeds and basal offsets

PLANT PARTNERS
Bush Clematis (*C. heracleifolia
davidiana*), Japanese Painted Fern
(*Athyrium goeringianum*)

Evolution is sometimes too much with us. It is so easy and convenient to slip into the hybrid thrall and put aside plants of subtle features and delicate nuance. A case in point is the family of foxgloves, so wild and unconstrained, they had no botanical name until 1542 when *Digitalis* was selected from the Latin word *digitus*, meaning "finger." The common name of foxglove is drawn from the Anglo-Saxon *foxes glofa*, meaning "fox gloves," alluding to the legend that bad fairies gave these flowers or "gloves" to the fox, that he might put them on his toes and silently steal into the chicken roost. The leaves of foxglove contain powerful cardiac stimulants that can be fatal if ingested, which in Ireland gave it the popular name of dead man's thimbles.

Garden luminaries in the 20th century were captured by the biennial foxglove hybrids of the Shirley and Excelsior strains, with great flaring Technicolor bells standing straight out in heraldic fashion and encircling 360 degrees of the stems. They are fabulous to see, but one keeps waiting for the blast of fanfare, as they give the impression of being plugged in. In a rare instance of familiarity breeding contempt, Vita Sackville-West was momentarily swayed by the new monstrous flower spikes growing to 7 feet (2 m), which she described as "far superior to the woodland foxglove, flowering all round the stem, and in colours preferable to the old magenta, lovely as they may look in the woods." Some of us liked the old magenta just fine, thank you.

The foxgloves of woodland glens and wet meadows are shy sorts with their bells hanging provocatively along one side of the 4- to 5-foot (120 to 150 cm) stem, as if they had a preference for that aspect. The common purple foxglove (*D. purpurea*) has tender rosy-mauve bells reminiscent of gloxinias and with a scattering of dark markings just inside the throat, each dark blotch surrounded with a pale band of milky white. The spots are similar to the markings on butterfly wings and on the tails of peacocks and pheasants, and are markers for bees and other friendly pollinators. *D. purpurea* is meant to be a self-seeding biennial, sending up its flower stalk from last year's rosette of leaves, but often turns perennial if the situation suits it. Some bloom reliably for many years in gardens with moist, woodsy soil, and the best advice is to leave them undisturbed — movement could change their contented disposition. There is a white variety (*D. purpurea* 'Alba') that is quite beautiful although it does lack the throat spots.

Seeds of white plants will usually revert to their pink or purple ancestors if pollinated by a bee that has visited a purple plant. To build a good stand of them, immediately remove any purple plants as soon as they show color, leaving only the white plants to pollinate each other. And there is another close cousin, *D. mertonensis*, the strawberry foxglove with a color described as like crushed berries, although in reality it is more muted.

Thankfully, the genes that came together in foxgloves also went in some other interesting directions. The yellow foxgloves, *D. grandiflora*, are reliably perennial and send up 3-foot (90 cm) stalks with nodding tubes or bells of pleasant straw yellow, sometimes with a freckling of brown spots in the throat. They form little offshoots at the base that can be separated in early spring to increase the planting. A similar cousin, *D. lutea*, is referred to as the smaller yellow foxglove and leads to some confusion. It is a bit more delicate and some would say refined, but that is not in any way an objective remark. Despite their reputation for growing in shady places, foxgloves of all sorts are quite happy to excel and grow an extra foot in full sun if the soil is consistently moist and full of good organic material. Removing the seed capsules before they develop helps to extend bloom for six weeks. Their basal rosettes make attractive foliage clumps and are almost evergreen, bearing an amazing amount of frost while remaining green. There are several more exotic species and one worth having is *D. ferruginea*, the rusty foxglove, with attractive lance-like 6-inch (15 cm) leaves and a tall slender flower spike carrying stylized pale yellow bells with dark markings.

Who could turn their back on these tender foxglove bells? Digitalis purpurea is *sometimes perennial, sometimes biennial, but usually leaves a few seedlings so we are never without. The interesting spots are bee-signage advertising a private roll-about in each foxy bell.*

Golden Marguerite
Master Goodyer's Escape

PLANT
Golden Marguerite,
Anthemis tinctoria

OTHER NAMES
Dyer's Chamomile, Ox-Eye
Chamomile

BLOOM
June to August

SIZE
Height 2 feet (60 cm),
width 2 to 3 feet (60 to 120 cm)

FORM
Loose clump

HARDINESS
Zone 4, hardy to –30°F (–34°C)

LOCATION
Full sun

SOIL
Average garden soil, well drained

WATER
Slightly dry

PROPAGATION
Root division, seeds

PLANT PARTNERS
Pincushion Flower
(*Scabiosa caucasica*), Big Betony
(*Stachys grandiflora*)

Among the herbal plants long associated with gardens and homes is golden marguerite (*Anthemis tinctoria*), a member of the chamomile family, which itself has a long history of usefulness. Chamomile was cultivated from before 1265 in Britain, where it is native, as a plant "to warme and comfort, and to ease paines being applied outwardly, after many fashions…"(John Parkinson, *Paradisi*). Its secondary use was as a groundcover for lawns, banks, and alleys, from which we have the chamomile lawn, such as the one that was for many years maintained within the grounds of Buckingham Castle.

The golden marguerite, *Anthemis tinctoria*, is a captivating little daisy plant of great value to gardeners, for it is entirely undemanding and will settle in wherever there is bright light. But in a previous life it was known as dyer's chamomile and contributed its flowers to making a bright yellow pigment used to color fabric. It was first grown by the eminent botanist John Goodyer, who was untiring in his search for new and useful plants. Goodyer's reputation was so esteemed that during the English civil war a royalist general ordered his men "on all occasions to defend and protect John Goodyer, his house, servants, family, goods, chattels and estates of all sorts from all damages, disturbances and oppressions whatever." It would appear Goodyer's house and gardens were all that was left standing in the village, which says something about the horticultural professions.

Goodyer describes the leaves of golden marguerite as "finlie jagged and minced like the leaves of tansie but much smaller…the flowers not onlie haveing a great yealowe ball are likewise of a bright yealowe color and are finely nickt at the toppe and commonlie two, three, four, or five and twentie in number." Which does quite well to describe the flowers of *A. tinctoria* as we know them. Of course this is one of the plants daisy lovers can't get enough of, and fortunately it produces masses of stems ideal for cutting.

Golden marguerite likes a dryish soil with good drainage and shouldn't be given fertilizer, which only causes the stems to elongate and topple over. It blooms from late spring to late summer, and even longer if deadheaded regularly. Golden marguerites can exhaust themselves with blooming and may die out in the center of the clump, but they will set replacement shoots from their central crown, and these can be separated and grown on to flowering size. There are several color combinations for the little daisies, and it's very nice to have more than one in the garden. 'E.C. Buxton' has 1- to 2-inch (2.5 to 5 cm) daisy flowers, off-white rays surrounding lemon yellow centers, held on stiff stems with their faces turned upward to light. 'Beauty of Grallach' is entirely deep golden, and 'Grallach Gold' has orange-tipped yellow flowers on $2^1/2$ foot (75 cm) plants. 'Kelwayi' is entirely yellow and 18 to 24 inches (45 to 60 cm) tall. The pale colors are light yellow 'Moonlight' and butter-yellow-fading-to-ivory 'Pale Moon', which grows to 24 inches (60 cm).

A ribbon of golden marguerite, the dyer's chamomile, meanders through Turid Forsyth's garden. The flowers give a deep yellow dye used to color fabric and wool yarn.

Speedwell
The Minx Plant

PLANT
Speedwell, *Veronica spicata*,
V. longifolia

OTHER NAMES
Common Gypsyweed, Paul's Betony

BLOOM
June to August

SIZE
Height 12 to 48 inches (30 to
120 cm), spread 12 to 24 inches
(30 to 60 cm)

FORM
Open clump with flower spikes

HARDINESS
Zone 3, hardy to –40°F (–40°C)

LOCATION
Full sun

SOIL
Well-drained garden soil with aged
manure

WATER
Moist in spring, will tolerate drought
thereafter

PROPAGATION
Root division in spring, stem cuttings
in summer

PLANT PARTNERS
Rose Campion (*Lychnis coronaria*),
Yellow Loosestrife (*Lysimachia
punctata*)

Certain plants make a point of keeping themselves to themselves, perhaps to avoid the eventual attention of hybridizers. One thinks of the roses and peonies which became the focus of early breeding schemes. If they could have an opinion, would they have chosen otherwise? Although an ancient plant with therapeutic uses, speedwell managed to elude organized study for quite a while by metamorphosing into a diverse range of species with disparate characteristics. Their varying heights, habits of growth, and flowering times confused the old herbalists, and as one authority says, "They appear under strange disguises, such as Blue Willow-herb, among members of the Onagraceae, or Wild Germander, mixed up with the Labiates" (Alice M. Coats, *Flowers and Their Histories*, 1956). Well, more power to them.

It's no surprise that confusion exists in the origin of the plant's name. Some believe *Veronica* is derived from the Greek words *phero*, "I bring," and *nike*, "victory," a reference to its medicinal efficacy. (*Veronica* was used as an expectorant, and there is no doubt it caused a great deal to be coughed up.) But others say it was named for the early Christian, St. Veronica, or perhaps the words *vera icon*, meaning "true image." Veronica gave Jesus Christ a towel to wipe his face on the way to Cavalry, where he was executed, leaving an image of himself on the cloth. Certainly the Victorians subscribed to that version of events, for in their language of flowers speedwell represents female faithfulness.

The speedwells are plants of mountains, meadows, and thin woods, places where they can go about their business with little interference. Many have been known as "minx plants," a polite synonym for weeds, among them *V. filiformis*, creeping veronica, which the shade gardener George Schenk says is "all too growable…(and) gets into lawns and makes them so despisedly beautiful with that light blue sky of flowers hazing the grass over in April and May." More constrained is *V. repens*, a ground-hugging perennial for part shade that forms mats with small pale blue flowers in late spring. Another species worth having in the garden is the gentian speedwell, *V. gentianoides*, which arrived from the Caucasus in 1784. It has small leaves 2 to 3 inches (5 to 7.5 cm) long and delicate flower spikes reaching 24 inches (60 cm) high with dense terminal clusters of pale mauve flowers in summer.

The showiest speedwells are the products of the hybridizers' work, and it has been well worth the effort to corral two of these wayward species. *Veronica spicata* hybrids are 12 to 18 inches (30 to 45 cm) tall with vibrant colors like the white 'Icicle', glowing cherry red 'Red Fox', and lavender 'Blue Charm'. Taller plants come from *V. longifolia*, with flower spikes ranging from 2 to 4 feet (60 to 120 cm) in height. This group includes 'Sunny Border Blue', which has won awards for its steady supply of bold blue flower spikes over six to eight weeks in summer. Speedwells need bright sun to produce the maximum numbers of flower spikes, in a location with well-drained soil. They love heat and will tolerate short summer droughts, and as with all perennials, removing the spent flowers prolongs blossoming.

5

MID- TO LATE SEASON
blooms

"...for me August is the full-blown month.
The year is full open and ripe and about to
seed. With its yucca towers of bells, its
hollyhocks and agapanthus, its exotic tall
petunias and glowing regiments of dahlias,
its burning zinnias and fuchsias, above all,
perhaps, with its drowsy companies of
butterflies tumbling all the hot day on the
buddleia flowers, it is a month of blowing beauty."

H.E. BATES, IN THE HEART OF THE COUNTRY

Balloon Flower
The Flower of Our Inner Child

PLANT
Balloon Flower,
Platycodon grandiflorus

OTHER NAMES
Chinese Bellflower

BLOOM
July to September

SIZE
Height 24 inches (60 cm),
width 24 inches (60 cm)

FORM
Open clump

HARDINESS
Zone 3, hardy to –40°F (–40°C)

LOCATION
Part shade to full sun

SOIL
Well-drained, average to rich soil

WATER
Consistent moisture, will not
tolerate soggy soil

PROPAGATION
Division, seeds

PLANT PARTNERS
English Lavender
(*Lavandula angustifolia*),
Yarrow (*Achillea millefolium*)

The balloon flower is regarded with much affection by children who love to pop the swollen flower buds, and adults who remember the pleasure of doing so. The garden luminary Vita Sackville-West grew up in the Castle of Knoll, but pomp and circumstance didn't preclude her enjoyment of the simple blue flower, like "a tiny lantern, so tightly closed as though its little seams had been stitched together, with the further charm that you can pop it…if you are so childishly minded." Which clearly she was.

A German naturalist, Johann Georg Gmelin, conducting botanical exploration at the behest of the Russian Empress Anne, brought the blue balloon flowers, a close relative of the campanula clan, out of Siberia in 1754. But the flowers were known for centuries in China, for the roots were used as a substitute for ginseng, "the most valued panacea of the East." It is said the balloon flower is as common in classical Asian legend and poetry as the rose or violet is in our own, and in autumn their colorful foliage makes a spectacle on certain Japanese moors. One wonders if the Chinese and Japanese were also balloon bud poppers, but it is not spoken of and we shall never know.

Balloon flower, *Platycodon grandiflorus*, takes its name from the Greek words *platys* ("broad") and *kodon* ("bell"). It will grow in partial shade or full sun and prefers organic soil that is slightly acid to neutral. It knows how to get on about its business with no fuss whatsoever, as long as it has decent drainage. The fleshy roots and crown are susceptible to rot if water is allowed to pool or linger in the soil with no way out. But that is a situation anyone would be ashamed of and, of course, will not exist in your garden. The plants are among the latest to break ground in spring, so marking their spot is a smart way to prevent stray trowels from causing damage. Balloon flower's neat clumps are topped with the round "balloon" buds, and it should be said that pressing them to enjoy the crisp pop is likely to ruin the flower. Everyone will want to try it once, but then restraint is in order. Taking the time to remove faded blossoms will keep the plants producing flowers well into late summer and early autumn.

The clumps rarely need division, fortunately, because it is a tricky business that is best attempted in spring when the shoots are only a few inches high. The coarse roots are like stringy carrots and require deep digging to avoid injury. Balloon flowers are easy to start from seed, but their colors are not always consistent and purchased plants may be the

Here are two little balloon buds just ripe for popping, if anyone is so inclined. Balloon flower is slow to start in spring, but lasts a long time in bloom. It's also long lasting in a vase if the stem ends are seared in a flame or boiling water for 10 seconds to keep its sap in.

most expedient way to acquire good colors. There are innumerable named cultivars and Christopher Lloyd warns that the variety called 'Roseus', sometimes described as rosy pink, is a dirty and washed-out mauve. Unfortunately that cultivar also has a double, 'Roseus Plenus', that makes us want to take the risk. Blue 'Japonicus' has 10-lobed flowers, twice the normal number, and must give quite a whirly-gig effect. There are some dwarf varieties and several named pinks and whites, but blueness is what makes the balloon flower most special. They are very long-lasting when cut for a vase if the bottom of the cut stem is seared with a flame to prevent its sap from running out.

Black-Eyed Susan
The Upsala Daisy

PLANT
Black-Eyed Susan,
Rudbeckia fulgida, R. nitida

OTHER NAMES
Golden Coneflower, English
Bulls-Eye

BLOOM
July to October

SIZE
Height 2 to 6 feet (60 cm to 2 m),
spread 2 to 3 feet (60 to 90 cm)

FORM
Loose clumps with stiff flower stems

HARDINESS
Zone 4, hardy to –30°F (–34°C)

LOCATION
Part shade to full sun

SOIL
Average garden soil

WATER
Consistently moist, tolerates short
drought

PROPAGATION
Root division in spring

PLANT PARTNERS
Snow-on-the-Mountain (*Euphorbia marginata*, annual), Tiger Lily (*Lilium lancifolium*, hardy bulb)

We don't know who Susan was, but her flower always imparts happiness. The bright golden ray flowers with raised dark central cone were part of a passel of daisy-like flowers sent over to Europe before 1640, and Parkinson says they "came from the French colony about the river of Canada." There was an initial try-out with name selection, the first in 1635 being *Aconitum helianthemum canadense*, a mixture of monkshood and sunflower. Then the name was altered to *Doronicum americanum* or "Supposed Wolf's Bane of America." Finally, Linnaeus, the Swedish master botanist (1707–78), named it *Rudbeckia* after two Swedish botanists, father and son professors at the University of Upsala.

Olaf Rudbeck (the senior Rudbeck) founded the botanical garden at Upsala, where he grew many exotic plants and offered Linnaeus a position as tutor to his children. Linnaeus, who at that time was an impoverished student, had just introduced his theory on the sexuality of plants and was grateful for Rudbeck's support. The theory was that by counting male organs (pistils) and female organs (stamens), plants could be sorted into categories. Linnaeus further designated the pistils as husbands and the stamens as wives, with the whole flower representing the marriage bed. This graphic realism in the sex lives of flowers was too much for establishment authorities, and by 1808 the Bishop of Carlisle was of the opinion that "nothing could equal the gross prurience of Linnaeus's mind."

Rudbeckias are easy plants to grow in almost any situation. The stiff, slightly hairy stems hold the flowers high in all weathers, and each stem branches to carry several more 3- to 4-inch (8 to 10 cm) daisies. Average garden soil in full sun or part shade grows strong plants that open from July through to October. Consistently moist soil will ensure good blossoming for the longest possible time. *Rudbeckia fulgida* var. *sullivantii* 'Goldsturm' is an award-winning plant that grows to 24 inches (60 cm) tall and has stylized strap-like petals that are slightly reflexed. 'Goldsturm' fits well into any bed with other perennials. It spreads slowly from creeping roots but isn't an invasive plant. *Rudbeckia nitida* 'Herbstonne' is a tall plant growing to 6 feet (2 m) high, with quite large golden flowers and prominent raised cones. It is a showy plant good for placing next to the stairway of a wood deck or at the corner of a house.

Linnaeus's theory of plant sex is no longer considered reprehensible, but we do take offense at the introduction of silly plants. *Rudbeckia occidentalis* 'Green Wizard' is possibly the ugliest flower ever seen and should be relegated to the category of plants that have fallen off the back of a truck. It has bright green sepals sticking out like spikes around a large black cone, with no petals whatsoever, and looks more like a fishing lure than a flower. 'Green Wizard' is the kind of breeding monstrosity that provokes hissy fits in gardeners, although it does provide dramatic material for floral arrangers. We could probably do without the theatrics.

Rudbeckias are never subtle, but they do bloom for six to eight weeks. Most will slowly move outward, sending up a few shoots outside of the clump. Flowers with prairie heritage have great durability, and they also are long lasting in a vase.

Blanket Flower
The Streets of Gold Paving

PLANT
Blanket Flower,
Gaillardia × *grandiflora*,
G. pulchella (*G. drummondi*)

OTHER NAMES
Indian Blanket

BLOOM
July to September

SIZE
Height 2 to 3 feet (60 to 90 cm),
width 2 feet (60 cm)

FORM
Sprawling clump

HARDINESS
Zone 3, hardy to –40°F (–40°C)

LOCATION
Full sun

SOIL
Loose, well drained, sandy

WATER
Dryish, tolerates drought

PROPAGATION
Root division in spring, root cuttings,
seeds

PLANT PARTNERS
Gayfeather (*Liatris spicata*),
Perennial Flax (*Linum perenne*)

Just when you think the garden's color scheme is under control, a plant like blanket flower (more often known by its botanical name, *Gaillardia* × *grandiflora*) snags you at the garden center. Here is a color challenge, for *Gaillardia* is a plant of more colors than anyone has planned for. There are at least ten separate color combinations and two or more mixed series, and most of these cultivars are bi- or tri-colors in one flower, causing our color meters to throb with brightness.

Gaillardia is named for Gaillard de Charentonneau, an 18th-century French magistrate and botanical patron who sponsored plant-collecting expeditions. It is one of several golden, daisy-like composite flowers collected in North America and brought back to Europe. The British plant historian Alice M. Coats wrote, "We have received so many yellow-rayed composites — Coreopses, Heleniums, Rudbeckias, Heliopses, Sunflowers and Goldenrods — that we might be justified in believing that continent to be paved in gold." Can you see Miss Coats's image of boulevard plantings several feet deep with golden daisies, and all of us shading our eyes from the glare? For indeed it must have been puzzling to Britons, confined to an island nation, to grasp the diverse scope of North American topography and regions where so many brightly colored daisy flowers could roam at will, with never a clash in color or temperament.

Being such a large family of flowers, *Gaillardia* can also cause some confusion. Modern plants are developed from two species — perennial blanket flower, *G. aristata*, and its annual counterpart, *G. pulchella* (sometimes listed as *G. drummondi*). Consequently there are perennial and annual plants available for sale in spring and we must be clear about which we want. The perennial *G. aristata* cultivars are somewhat bigger, 2 to 3 feet (60 to 90 cm) in height with erect and sprawling stems, and of course they will return each year. The annual *G. pulchella* varieties are $1^1/2$ to 2 feet (45 to 60 cm) high with a neater round habit, and they will last one growing season. Their smaller demeanor makes them useful for planting up a container with heat-loving herbs such as purple basil and lavender; their neatness is useful for filling a small bed or lining a walk.

The common name blanket flower of course reflects the Native American heritage of blanket making, and the vibrant colors incorporated in that craft. The brightness of

With silvery Artemis to cool them off, blanket flowers flaunt their burnt sienna stamens. Keeping up with deadheading will bring on more weeks of flowers.

Gaillardia is set off by the cooler tones of pale thread leaf coreopsis (*Coreopsis verticillata*), tall 'Blue Horizon' ageratum, 'Blue Clips' campanula, purple coneflowers, and blue fescue. Both perennial and annual forms of the plant want a loose gravelly soil with not too much fertility or moisture. They will continue blooming even without deadheading and can stand up to heat and wind in exposed areas.

Delphinium
The Butterfly Brigade

PLANT
Delphinium,
Delphinium × belladonna

OTHER NAMES
Larkspur, Lark's Heel

BLOOM
July to September

SIZE
Height 3 to 7 feet (90 cm to 2 m),
width 18 to 36 inches (45 to 90 cm)

FORM
Multi-branched stems from a central
crown

HARDINESS
Zone 3, hardy to −40°F (−40°C)

LOCATION
Part shade to full sun

SOIL
Rich and organic, amended with
aged manure

WATER
Consistently moist, will not tolerate
drought

PROPAGATION
Root division in spring or autumn,
seeds

PLANT PARTNERS
Colewort (*Crambe cordifolia*),
Maltese Cross (*Lychnis
chalcedonica*)

Mention delphiniums and immediately the image of 7-foot (2 m) flower stalks packed with azure blue petals flashes across the mind of every gardener. That is the predictable reaction to this gorgeous plant that is desirable to many, but the growing success of only a few. For surely everyone knows that such tall flower stalks are a tragedy waiting to happen and bound to end in tears with the first big wind or pounding rain. Fortunately we are not without alternatives, for delphiniums have proven to be malleable material for the plant breeder's art.

Delphiniums take their name from the Greek word *delphis*, which means "dolphin," because the immature flower buds are thought to resemble that creature. Some plant historians argue the buds are more like tadpoles, but it seems an unnecessary distinction. The flowers were first cultivated in Italy about 1550 and called Stavesaker (*D. staphisagris*). The species was beautiful but gravely poisonous and was used with extreme caution; it was dried, powdered, and strewn on children's hair to eliminate head lice, which John Hill (*Eden; or a Compleat Body of Gardening*, 1757) noted, "never fails."

Various forms of annual delphinium, or larkspur as it is called, were grown in England, where it was valued as a wound herb and an enhancement to eyesight. The species *D. consolida* and *D. ajacis* were popular garden plants and grown in single, double, and variegated forms with many colors. Of course these were just the swelling wave to the real event, the introduction of *D. elatum*, first of the perennial plants from Siberia early in the 17th century. The Siberian delphinium was one of the important parents of the exhibition strains we know today, and it was crossbred with various other species for 250 years until it fell into the hands of that famous firm, Blackmore and Langdon, in 1907. And it could be said after that, there was nowhere to go but up.

Standard size delphiniums grow 5 to 8 feet (1.5 to 2.5 m) tall and have one request, and that is for a decent meal. They are often described, along with roses, as "gross feeders," and that means they want a bed prepared with one or two rich amendments such as garden compost, aged manure, alfalfa weed, kelp meal, bloodmeal, or bonemeal. Promptly cutting down the flower stalk after blooming and providing a feeding of commercial fertilizer or bloodmeal may result in a second bloom in September. But some gardeners prefer less formal and less accident-prone delphiniums, and Gertrude

Jekyll was one of them. "For my liking," she wrote, "the spike must be well filled but not overcrowded. Many of the show kinds are too full for beauty; the shape of the individual flower is lost….Though weak in growth, the old *Delphinium Belladonna* has so lovely a quality of color that it is quite indispensable" (*Wood and Garden: Notes and Thoughts, Practical and Critical, of a Working Amateur,* 1910).

The plant Miss Jekyll referred to is the lovely collection of butterfly delphiniums. The origin of the butterfly species is not known, but named varieties were produced from 1890 onwards. They grow in airy clumps of several branched stems reaching a height of 3 feet (90 cm), their flower stalks graced by showy clusters of informal, bright blue flowers. *Delphinium belladonna* has been considerably improved since Miss Jekyll's time and comes in three colors — deep blue 'Bellamosum', pure white 'Casa Blanca', and rosy 'Pink Sensation',

Turid Forsyth gambles and wins with these 'Pacific Giants' delphiniums. They are tall enough that wind could knock them down. But good soil moisture has kept the stalks straight and steady.

as well as mixed colors such as the white and light and dark blue 'Blue Fountain' series that can be grown from seed. They require a full sun position and will bloom for an extended period of eight weeks that can be prolonged by removing the spent flowering branches.

Other strong delphiniums with low height are the *D. belladonna* 'Connecticut Yankee' series with white and shades of blue flowers growing on bushy plants to 30 inches (75 cm). The 'Magic' series in 'Magic Dark Blue', 'Magic Heavenly Blue', 'Magic Lilac-Rose', and 'Magic White' are new hybrids growing to 36 inches (90 cm). The smallest and newest plant is the Chinese delphinium, *D. grandiflorum* 'Blue Mirror', a gorgeous rich blue mound with ferny foliage that blooms madly from June into August and September if the spent flowers are deadheaded. All these new low-growing delphiniums are derived or inspired by the original flight of butterfly delphiniums that were the object of Miss Jekyll's affection. Clumps of delphiniums can last many years in the garden, providing they don't have water or ice lingering about their crowns to cause rot. Plant them in a slightly mounded bed to encourage drainage.

Globe Thistle
The Flower of Medieval Weaponry

PLANT
Globe Thistle, *Echinops ritro*

OTHER NAMES
Small Globe Thistle

BLOOM
July to September

SIZE
Height 5 feet (150 cm),
width 3 feet (90 cm)

FORM
Broad sprawling clumps

HARDINESS
Zone 4, hardy to –30°F (–34°C)

LOCATION
Full sun

SOIL
Average garden soil, well drained

WATER
Consistent moisture in spring,
tolerates drought

PROPAGATION
Division of basal offsets, seeds

PLANT PARTNERS
Maltese Cross
(*Lychnis chalcedonica*), Shasta Daisy
(*Chrysanthemum superbum*)

The dry hills of Spain and southern France have evolved some of our favorite plants, and among them is this large and willful clump of bristly leaves and spiky blue ball-flowers. Globe thistle is not a thistle at all, but does have similar prickly foliage and a dominant disposition. It is a plant for a big space alongside a sunny fence with a climbing pink rose or sprawl of honeysuckle vine, or positioned at the foot of a country driveway in the company of yellow daylilies.

Echinops takes its name from the Greek words *echinos*, meaning "hedgehog," and *ops*, "appearance," a reference to the densely packed round flowers with deceptively sharp-looking points. Its deeply incised leaves grow 3 feet high (90 cm) and the steel-blue flower spikes rise another 2 feet (60 cm) above the foliage from June to September. These perfectly round ball-shaped flowers bounce about in the wind and are intriguing to watch. Eleanor Perenyi (*Writer in the Garden*, 1981) said they are like "the weapons one sees in the medieval armory." If the flowers are cut just as they reach full color, they can be dried for long-lasting winter arrangements, but if left to mature on the plant they will shatter. There are several related species of *Echinops*, all with an inclination to lean and flop over as the season progresses. The disorganized demeanor of the clump is part of its charm, for it is constantly moving like a restless sleeper and is suitable in a relaxed or naturalized setting where its strong texture and frosty blue flowers can stand out. Two hybrids worth pursuing are powdery steel blue 'Taplow Blue' and the darker 'Veitch's Blue'.

Globe thistle grows best in full sun and well-drained soil. It doesn't require fertilizing and will sow just a few of its own seeds to provide occasional new plants. Offsets can also be separated from its base in spring. *Echinops* is a plant of strong visual character, but not everyone appreciates its diversity. Christopher Lloyd was peeved when he wrote that "its prickly green foliage is distinguished for being exceptionally undistinguished." But William Robinson said it is "a fine hardy plant…the most ornamental of its distinct family, and is highly suitable for grouping with the bolder herbaceous plants. It would also look well when isolated on the turf." Go figure.

Globe thistles congregate like a gathering of errant knights, their globular blossoms jousting in the breeze. Despite their spiky appearance, the flowers are spine-less and good for drying. The round, sphere-shaped flower form is called pseudocephalia, *a word to be used at your peril.*

Gooseneck Loosestrife
Animal Strategies

PLANT
Gooseneck Loosestrife, *Lysimachia clethroides*

OTHER NAMES
Japanese Loosestrife, Gooseneck Plant

BLOOM
July to September

SIZE
Height 3 to 4 feet (90 to 120 cm), width 3 feet (90 cm)

FORM
Tall, erect clump

HARDINESS
Zone 4, hardy to -30°F (-34°C)

LOCATION
Partial shade to full sun

SOIL
Organic woodland soil

WATER
Consistently moist, tolerates short drought

PROPAGATION
Root division

PLANT PARTNERS
Gayfeather (*Liatris spicata*), Hungarian Speedwell (*Veronica latifolia*)

Depending on whom you talk to, gooseneck loosestrife is either an elegant asset in the perennial border or a bold interloper. The discrepancy in opinion has to do with perspective and whether the glass is half full or half empty. Yes, it is an elegant plant, holding its stems with proud posture and sense of purpose, and draping lovely white goosey flowers into a provocative flounce. And yes, it has a rhizomatous root system with a propensity to run in ideal soil conditions. But rather than be a ninny and throw the baby out with the bath water, surely there is an accommodation to be found.

Lysimachia clethroides is a plant of Asian origin and, of all things, a member of the primrose family, a distinction hard to recognize in its demeanor. It is named in deference to King Lysimachos of Thrace (c. 360–281 B.C.), who was an animal strategist and settled a quarrel between two yoked oxen by laying a stalk of loosestrife across their shoulders, or so Pliny said. Why any animal could be distracted from argument in that manner remains a mystery. And so the plants of this family are associated with reconciliation and negotiation, qualities always welcome in the garden.

Gooseneck loosestrife supports its stems firmly for the whole season and has a blooming period of six weeks. It prefers moist soil and flowers well in part sun, part shade situations and will endure a short drought. If moved into full sun, it needs its soil to be consistently moist, as too much heat and drought stress can cause it to cease flowering. Gardeners have some little tricks to keep the roots from making large strides. Some grow the plant in dry shade, which tends to discourage spreading. Others set a plastic collar in place around the plant, corralling the root system for several years. And some use a spade in spring to take a bit away all around the clump and keep it in bounds. Any of these techniques seems a small price to pay for such a large and fine plant that puts on a first-rate display late into the season. Giving it some room to spread seems yet another option, resulting in more of a good thing.

The lysimachias are a diverse group. The yellow loosestrife, *L. punctata*, is a stiff and sturdy 3-foot (90 cm) plant with "cheap and cheerful" small yellow flowers in late spring. *L. nummularia* is a trailing deep green wanderer only 2 inches (5 cm) high. Both are useful plants, but neither has the elegance or desirability of their gooseneck

Sometimes called shepherd's crook but more often known as gooseneck loosestrife, this fetching plant is an old-fashioned favorite. Moist soil makes it invasive; dryer soil keeps it in one place.

cousin. Gooseneck loosestrife looks good with other plants of similar stature, such as bee balms (*Monarda*), globe thistle (*Echinops*), and sneezeweed (*Helenium*).

Hollyhocks
The Flower of Sleeping Bees

The sitting down, when school was o'er
Upon the threshold of the door,
Picking from Mallows, sport to please,
The crumpled seed we called a cheese.

THE SHEPHERD'S CALENDAR — JOHN CLARE (1793–1864)

PLANT
Hollyhock, *Althaea rosea*
(or *Alcea rosea*)

OTHER NAMES
Cheeses, Outlandish Rose, Rosa
Ultramarina

BLOOM
July to September

SIZE
Height 6 to 8 feet (2 to 2.5 m),
width 3 feet (90 cm)

FORM
Broad clump with flower stalk

HARDINESS
Zone 4, hardy to –30°F (–34°C)

LOCATION
Full sun

SOIL
Well-drained garden soil with aged
manure

WATER
Consistently moist through summer

PROPAGATION
Seeds sown in July

PLANT PARTNERS
Baby's Breath
(*Gypsophila paniculata*), Sea Holly
(*Eryngium* × *zabelii*)

Seldom has there been a flower so evocative of time and place. One sees hollyhocks and thinks of country lanes, cottage gardens, and white picket fences by the sea. The nodding clusters of multi-colored stems, some towering 7 or 8 feet (2 or 2.5 m), are like crazy quilt patterns or, as the American garden author Louise Beebe Wilder said, "an effect of old-fashioned chintz." But despite these close-to-home images, *Althaea rosea* is indigenous to Asia and the arid Holy Land, and is the largest of the ornamental plants in the ancient mallow family. The word *holy-hocke* appears in John Gardiner's poem *Feate of Gardening* (1440), indicating the plant was already cultivated in Britain. *Hoc* refers to the Anglo-Saxon word for a mallow, and it is likely that the hollyhock was found growing wild in Palestine by Crusaders and brought home in saddlebags. The plant historian Alice M. Coats says it was lost and found several times over, "but at the most conservative estimate, it has a garden history extending over more than five hundred years."

It is difficult to overlook a hollyhock at the height of July in full flight of blossoms, and they have loomed large and with indiscriminate ease in cottage borders and aristocratic beds. The country folk called them by the name "cheese," referring to the tight round seed capsules resembling wheels of cheese made in home dairies. Double as well as single forms have been grown since earliest times, and the botanist John Parkinson described a double blossom early in the 17th century as "a darke red like blacke bloud," certainly a color that would be popular now with the revival of black-flushed flowers. In fact, he may have been speaking of the black hollyhock, *Althaea nigra*, the deepest maroon-black hollyhock still with us. One garden planner for the carriage trade (John

In gardens where rust plagues hollyhocks, this Siberian native, the Antwerp or fig-leaved hollyhock (Althaea ficifolia), is a disease-resistant alternative. The three-lobed leaf is characteristic of this strain of single flowers.

Lawrence, 1726) suggested hollyhocks were "fittest for courts or spatious gardens, being soe great and stately, or the Corners of Gardens should be assigned to them, where they may explain their Beauty to distant Views."

Of course these days some of us have forgotten how to appreciate hollyhocks, and we are more likely to find a glorious clump of them in an alley bursting from cracked concrete, or alongside a gas station garage. The Victorians were very fond of the flowers, which were removed from the stems and sold commercially by florists. In Gertrude Jekyll's garden the hollyhocks were intensively tended and the stalks were prevented from leaning with 4-foot (120 cm) stakes holding them straight up in an enchanted forest effect. Larger blooms were produced by topping the plants, that is, stopping their upward growth by snipping off the top foot of the flower stalk and driving the energy back down into the lower blooms. The floral trade suddenly collapsed with the arrival of hollyhock rust in about 1870, an insidious fungus disease as destructive as potato blight and caused by the organism *Puccinia malvacearum*, which disfigures the leaves with orange spots and terminates flower production.

The double Chater's Strain of perennial hollyhocks is an opulent collection of bomb-type blossoms developed by Mr. W. Chater, who planted and bred an acre of plants at Saffron Walden in the 1880s. His hybrids surpassed the number of dahlia cultivars available, and some of the exhibition hybrids included an elegantly pale 'Double Apricot' and dark sable 'Black Prince', both still available today. The problem with hollyhock rust exists in some gardens, but can be strategically overcome by growing the disease-resistant variety, *Althaea ficifolia*, the fig-leaved or Antwerp hollyhock (originally from Siberia). It is a more freely branching plant with lower height (about 5 feet/150 cm) and produces widely flared and ruffled single flowers that bumblebees fall asleep in. Does anyone need reminding that bumblebees live a solitary existence apart from hive colonies and are docile creatures? They fly quite late in the early evening, as long as there is a bit of daylight, and they have a special passion for hollyhocks. But when temperatures drop quickly at sundown, the chill immobilizes the bees and the flower closes around them for the night. An early-morning tour of the garden will reveal these fuzzy fellows still asleep as the flowers open to dawn light.

Hollyhocks are capable of growing just about anywhere there is full sunlight, but will produce more flowers over a period of six to eight weeks if their soil is moist and rich. If the plants finish blossoming early, cut the flower stalks back and provide some fertilizer for a potential second blooming. Hollyhocks grow easily from seed started in July for blooms the following year, and the strongest plants are produced from seeds sown directly into the bed. Some plants are biennial, but in ideal conditions will convert to perennial behavior. Large clumps produce side shoots at the base that can be separated and set on their own to quickly mature.

Musk Mallow
The French Druggists' Plant

What a confusion of riches are the mallows. They are the most obliging plants, giving us their best in simple flared flowers along extending stems from July to frost, or rocketing up gracefully like the hollyhock, their largest cousin. The musk mallow, *Malva moschata*, is at the core of traditional cottage garden plantings, with its 2-inch (5 cm) pale silky white or pink blossoms on spreading 24-inch (60 cm) stems. There is warm debate over whether this is a garden plant that has escaped into the wild, or a wildling that has leaped into the border. Really, the matter of direction cannot be resolved, but we are just so pleased to have it with us. William Robinson (*The English Flower Garden*, 1883) noted, "One of the best is the white variety of the native Musk Mallow, *M. moschata*...worth growing with *M. alcea*...in a full collection." It's interesting that he didn't disqualify the musk mallow in favor of its slightly more sophisticated cousin, the hollyhock mallow, and clearly each had sufficient value in his collection.

Malva moschata has long been used by country people as a medicinal plant, for the roots contain a mucilaginous juice that has soothing qualities for teething babies and all manner of inflammations. Mrs. M. Greve (*A Modern Herbal*, 1931) says, "French druggists and English sweet-meate makers prepare a confectionary paste (*Pate de Guimauve*) from the roots of Mallow, which is emollient and soothing to a sore chest, and valuable in coughs and hoarseness. The 'Marsh Mallows' usually sold by confectioners here are a mixture of flour, gum, egg-albumin, etc., and contain no mallow." And so we see how a simple folk remedy leapt into the realm of multimillion-dollar confectionery and campfire tradition.

The true hollyhock is the largest of the ornamental mallows, but the scaled-down version, the hollyhock mallow, *M. alcea* var. *fastigiata*, is an essential plant in any long-blooming perennial border. It makes a bushy mound of pink 2- to 3-inch (5 to 7.5 cm) flowers around a white center, each flower appearing in the leaf axil as it meets the central stems. By midsummer hollyhock mallow is 48 inches (120 cm) high and by cutting back the stems with finished flowers, it will continue to pump out blossoms until frost. The species plant is a soft pink, and the variety *fastigiata* is deeper tones with a fine

PLANT
Musk Mallow, *Malva moschata*, *M. alcea* var. *fastigiata*

BLOOM
July to September

SIZE
Height 2 to 3 feet (60 to 90 cm), spread 2 to 3 feet (60 to 90 cm)

FORM
Sprawling clump

HARDINESS
Zone 4, hardy to –30°F (–34°C)

LOCATION
Full sun

SOIL
Average garden soil, well drained

WATER
Consistently moist, tolerates drought

PROPAGATION
Stem cuttings, seeds

PLANT PARTNERS
Sundrops (*Oenothera tetragona*), Baby's Breath (*Gypsophila paniculata*)

It's hard to imagine these simple flowers were the inspiration for campfire marshmallows. The deeply cut foliage and soft rose pink to pale pink blossoms grow wild in the hedgerows of Britain.

carmine line in each petal. Mallows are tap-rooted plants and difficult to transplant or divide, but will make a modest amount of seedlings nearby that can be moved while still very young. Cuttings from stem tips can be taken in early summer and rooted for blossoming plants next year. Any plant with so many flowers benefits from consistent watering, but hollyhock mallow will tolerate some drought if necessary. But too much drought shortens the blooming length of every plant, so providing regular water is worth the effort.

Perennial Salvia
The Flower of Velvety Violence

The salvias came to us as medicinal plants in the centuries before the distinction between useful and ornamental plants was clearly drawn. Salvia was spoken of as "Sage the Savior," a reference to the plant's botanical name, which is derived from the Latin word *salvere*, meaning "to be saved." An old French saying confirms the public confidence in the plant's efficacy — "Sage helps the nerves and by its powerful might, Palsy is cured and fever put to flight."

Although many species of sage were grown in physic gardens for their medicinal properties, their beauty wasn't wasted on the monks who tended them. The strong reds, blues, and purples of sage flowers were adopted for ornamental purposes, bred by growers and displayed as a new order in plant aesthetics. And that was all it took to initiate a litany of critical color-focused dialogue that continued into the 19th century. One author referred to ornamental sages as "loud summer varieties." The British social critic John Ruskin (1819–1900) disapproved of salvias, saying, "These exotic sages have no moderation in their hues.…The velvety violent blue of the one and scarlet of the other, seem to have no gradation and no shade. There's no colour that gives me such an idea of violence — a sort of rough angry scream — as that shade of blue.…" No wonder the man suffered recurrent attacks of insanity during his last years. It must have been the blue salvias that pushed him over the edge.

Now that we are reconciled to brilliantly colored flowers and even welcome jewel tones in our gardens, perennial *Salvia* × *superba* is a plant of consequence, for it has bred many wonderful cultivars for lasting summer display. Perennial salvia needs a bright position with good garden loam that is consistently moist. Although it has built-in tolerance of drought, it will stop flower production in dry soil. Christopher Lloyd grows *Salvia* × *superba* in his garden at Great Dixter and says, "Few perennials are longer in flower than this, especially if you deadhead the first crop," and the consistent removal of spent flower spikes is a familiar refrain in perennial plant culture. Older clumps can be divided after four or five years to keep them vigorous and producing lots of flower spikes.

For brightness you can't beat the violet sage 'May Night', which sends up flower spikes from a basal clump of leaves over a six-week season of bloom. The 18-inch

PLANT
Perennial Salvia, *Salvia* × *superba*

OTHER NAMES
Violet Sage

BLOOM
July to September

SIZE
Height 18 inches (45 cm),
width 18 inches (45 cm)

FORM
Tight slump with erect flower spikes

HARDINESS
Zone 4, hardy to –30°F (–34°C)

LOCATION
Full sun

SOIL
Average garden soil, well drained

WATER
Consistently moist, will tolerate
short drought

PROPAGATION
Root division, stem cuttings

PLANT PARTNERS
Chinese Delphinium (*Delphinium grandiflorum*), Purple Mullein (*Verbascum phoeniceum*)

The dusty purples spires of 'Purple Rain' salvia have a long bloom time through the heat of summer. Deadheading finished flower spikes once or twice triggers side shoots. Unlike other salvias, 'Purple Rain' is a sprawling plant good for slight slopes where it can cascade.

(45 cm) spikes are covered with small two-lipped flowers in rich, dark indigo-violet with reddish purple bracts. 'East Friesland' and the shorter 'Blue Queen' are also blue-violet cultivars, and 'Rose Queen' puts up 30-inch (75 cm) stems of rose-pink flowers. 'Lubecca' is another tall, 30-inch (75 cm) violet-blue salvia. But if anyone close by is feeling a bit like the unfortunate Mr. Ruskin, consider the softer tones of two German *S.* × *superba* hybrids, light-blue 'Blue Hill' and white 'Snow Hill', or possibly combine the softer tones with darker salvias for a completely mind-boggling effect.

Prairie Mallow
Lost in the West

PLANT
Prairie Mallow, *Sidalcea malviflora*

OTHER NAMES
Miniature Hollyhock,
Checkerbloom

BLOOM
July to September

SIZE
Height 3 to 4 feet (90 to 120 cm),
width 2 feet (60 cm)

FORM
Small basal rosette with tall flower
stems

HARDINESS
Zone 5, hardy to –20°F (–29°C)

LOCATION
Full sun

SOIL
Fertile, humus-rich, well drained

WATER
Consistently moist, doesn't tolerate
drought

PROPAGATION
Root division, seeds

PLANT PARTNERS
Spike Speedwell (*Veronica spicata*),
Beardtongue (*Penstemon barbatus*)

There's no telling what plants will get up to when left to ramble about alone for a few thousand years. Mostly they hybridize themselves quite well and adapt to wherever the wind takes them, although we do like to think nothing of merit happens outside of controlled greenhouse circumstances. But prairie mallow is a case in point, for it has been rolling along out in the moist mountain meadows of North America for quite some time, reeling off 25 species and breeding itself to produce some pretty, and marketable, flowers.

Catalogues of indigenous species plants and wildflowers list several of the wild sidalceas such as *S. neomexicana* and *S. oregana*, from fairly exotic locales like chaparral-creosote bush and coastal sage scrub environments. Occasionally someone notices what is going on and selects out a species to work with, and that is how two sidalceas came to be known in the gardening world beyond the mountains. *Sidalcea candida* 'Bianca' is a lovely spire of white blossoms, only occasionally seen. But *S. malviflora*, the prairie mallow, is more often available and a wonderful plant to have in the garden.

Prairie mallow is a scaled-down relation of the traditional hollyhock, and that is immediately apparent, for it sends up tall slender stems of hibiscus-like flowers from a low rosette of leaves. The flowers themselves also have the single outward facing countenance of hollyhock, but in an entirely smaller and more refined manner. *Sidalcea* is a charming cottage garden flower, making us think of summer lawn parties and hummingbirds buzzing the blossoms. It is at home in the civilized border with campanulas, summer phlox, pincushion flower, and the silver leaves of artemisia.

Extremes of heat and dryness are certain disaster for prairie mallow, for it likes a mild environment with warm days and cool evenings, and requires moist organic soil with good drainage in part shade to full sun. It's so dependent on moisture that the least drought will shut down flowering. Removing the spent flower stems works very well to keep this lovely plant blooming all summer. 'Party Girl' produces 2-inch (5 cm) rose flowers with white centers, standing about 3 feet (90 cm) tall. Deep red-rose 'Stark's Hybrid' and rose-pink 'Rose Queen' are the tallest sidalceas at 48 inches (120 cm). In between are shell-pink 'Loveliness' and salmon-pink 'William Smith', both growing to about 2^{1}/2 feet (75 cm).

Sidalcea oregana *is a western prairie mallow species that doesn't need much improvement. Nevertheless it is a partner in several hybrid prairie mallows. Side shoots bloom when the central spike is finished.*

Purple Coneflower
The Cult of Daisies

PLANT
Purple Coneflower,
Echinacea purpurea

OTHER NAMES
Black Sampson, Purple Rudbeckia

BLOOM
July to September

SIZE
Height 3 to 4 feet (90 to 120 cm),
spread 18 to 24 inches (45 to
60 cm)

FORM
Clump with vertical flower stalks

HARDINESS
Zone 3, hardy to –40°F (–40°C)

LOCATION
Part shade to full sun

SOIL
Average garden soil, well drained

WATER
Consistent moisture, will tolerate
short drought

PROPAGATION
Seeds, root division in spring

PLANT PARTNERS
Black-Eyed Susan (*Rudbeckia* spp.),
Balloon Flower (*Platycodon
grandiflorus*)

With little here to do or see
Of things that in the great world be,
Daisy! Again I talk to thee,
  For thou art worthy;
Thou unassuming commonplace
Of Nature, with that homely face
And yet with something of a grace,
  Which love makes for thee!

WILLIAM WORDSWORTH

You might think the purple coneflower is something new on the horizon, but it has been rattling around the prairies in the company of wild grasses for a very long time. Gardeners have been familiar with hybrid cultivars of *Echinacea purpurea* for the past two decades and could be forgiven for not recognizing its prairie cousin, narrowleaf echinacea (*E. angustifolia*). The strange narrowleaf coneflower is a true wildflower of dry woodlands and pastures, shaped like a shuttlecock with thin dusty-pink petals hanging starkly back from the raised central cone. Coneflowers purchased from a garden center are sure to be the brightly colored new hybrids, altogether sturdier, bigger, and more flamboyant than their shuttlecock cousin. And while they make a shameless display of form and sometimes garish color, they are disarming plants with no inhibitions, and gardeners who like them at all secretly admire their "in your face" attitude.

Although the prairie cousin is a less demonstrative plant in every way, it has been valued for its roots' superior chemical constituents, which are powerful boosters to the human immune system. North American native peoples used it for centuries to treat snakebites and infectious diseases, just as we make use of it in the prevention of colds. But it also had a high profile as a viable treatment for syphilis and was particularly useful to boatmen on the Missouri River who had "experienced unpleasant consequences from their intercourse with the Squaws" (*Travels into the Interior of America*, John

Bradbury, 1819). It is entirely likely the unpleasantness was something these fellows brought with them. However, it's quite a revelation that the herbal preparation we take routinely for cold prevention may provide treatments and safeguards we hadn't anticipated.

Purple coneflower is especially coveted by the cult of daisy-lovers, of which there are many. They are gardeners of joyful disposition, characterized by a love of any blossom with composite, daisy-like form. Large clumps and spreading drifts of daisy flowers are to be found wherever they wield influence and a trowel, and purple coneflowers fit perfectly into their plans. Coneflowers are happy in bright sun, although they will soldier on in part shade producing fewer flowers, and they like their soil to have a bit of enrichment with aged manure or compost. Coneflowers have some drought resistance inherited in their prairie genes, but will flower best if moisture is consistent. Individual flower stalks can reach 4 feet (120 cm), and the clumps can get big and resent movement. Initial spacing of 18 to 24 inches (45 to 60 cm) between plants is wise planning. Coneflowers don't divide well, but are easy to start from seed sown directly in the ground and also will seed themselves (although their progeny are usually more drab than the parent).

The colors of hybrid *Echinacea* plants could not be described as shy. 'Crimson Star' purple coneflower has deep rosy-purple ray petals that stand straight out (not hanging back, like the wild plants), surrounding a broad and prominent golden-brown center. 'Bright Star' has glowing rose-red petals and 'The King' has coral-crimson petals surrounding black-maroon centers, but 'Magnus' (also called 'Bravado' and 'Ovation') is quite toned down in comparison, a subdued pink that looks well alongside the pink shrub rose 'Royal Bonica'. These bright coneflowers teach us an interesting lesson in the triumph of irrepressible exuberance over predictable color choices. But for true style and elegance, none of the pink cultivars compares with the white coneflowers, 'White Swan' and 'White Lustre'. They have a statuesque bearing that emphasizes the purity of their white daisy petals and bronzy central disks, and just one plant at the corner of a border is enough to remind us that less is sometimes more in the garden.

The coneflowers show their prairie blood with rays bent back and cones upward, trolling for pollinators.

Summer Phlox
The Old-and-New-Again Flower

PLANT
Summer Phlox, *Phlox paniculata*

OTHER NAMES
Garden Phlox, Fall Phlox, Perennial Phlox

BLOOM
July to September

SIZE
Height 24 to 48 inches (60 to 120 cm), spread 24 inches (60 cm)

FORM
Tall clump with stiff erect stems

HARDINESS
Zone 3, hardy to -40°F (-40°C)

LOCATION
Part shade to full sun

SOIL
Rich organic loam, with aged manure

WATER
Consistently moist, won't tolerate drought

PROPAGATION
Root division in autumn or spring

PLANT PARTNERS
Aurelian Trumpet Lily (*Lilium* hybrids), Purple Coneflower (*Echinacea purpurea*)

Although we think of phlox as an old-fashioned flower, it is more a modern enthusiasm. Breeding work went on at a languorous pace, the plant first being grown as a mauve flower in England about 1732 in the garden of Dr. James Sherard at Eltham. Clearly the British were a bit indifferent, and it wasn't until 1812 that a white flower was produced, taking nearly a century to make a small and uncomplicated step forward. Finally the French hybridist M. Lierval jumped into the void with an accelerated breeding program, leaving the British in his tracks and supplying improved plants and new colors after 1839. It wasn't until late in that century that the British took interest again, and Captain Symons-Jeune began the work that would lead to the huge selection of cultivars after 1900.

There are several voices with something to say about phlox, and lest there be any confusion, it should be noted that the British do love phlox and consider it the backbone of every summer garden. Vita Sackville-West grew many full borders of phlox at Sissinghurst and was adamant that "they look better in isolation, closely packed…in a cool, north-aspect border, all to themselves, not mixed up with other things in a hot sunny border….It does give a sumptuous glowing show, especially if you can plant it in a half-shade bed where its colours will curiously change with the sinking sun and will deepen with twilight into colours you never thought it possessed." Now, could anyone remain unimpressed?

There is an interesting point to be taken about the rapid development of new phlox cultivars, and that is the "old" French cultivars (1840–1850) and new British (1890–1910) and then American cultivars were introduced so rapidly that all were available to gardeners at the same time, allowing for opportune comparisons. This has fostered debate about preferences for old versus new cultivars and also allowed something of a window on the science and art of plant hybridizing. Eleanor Perenyi (*The Writer in the Garden*, 1981) thought that "older hybrids are tougher than new ones: In my garden are two stands of pink phlox that are thirty-five years old. They start to bloom at the end of June and continue into September. The newer, flashier phloxes with larger flower trusses bloom six weeks later, and are far more subject to powdery mildew into the bargain."

Bright enough for you? Mildew problems can be prevented by removing some flower stems early on to create open spaces for air circulation.

A nerve was struck with the novelist and naturalist H.E. Bates (*A Love of Flowers*, 1971), who commented on "the detestable word 'cultivar,' which always sounds to me like an ugly Russian cross between 'samovar' and a collective farm. I consequently consign it to the muck-heap…where I hope it will rot." It seems unnecessary to have drawn the Russians into it, but he did have definite preference for a particular old hybrid, "*Phlox* 'Norah Leigh,'…a variegated phlox in light green and cream, an old plant rediscovered in a cottage garden, not grown for her flowers, which are of a rather insipid pink, but purely for foliage effect, which endures for weeks and weeks from May onwards." Bates was writing in 1969, and of course 'Norah Leigh' faded away and was discovered yet again in the mid-1990s, and no doubt will keep popping up for rediscovery every 30 years or so.

As Ms. Perenyi has said, the older phlox plants are earliest blooming, starting in late June and carrying on to early autumn. They have slightly smaller flower heads and a good range of colors, and are often scented. Phlox have a sweet scent with an underlying muskiness that the gardening author A.E. Bowles described as a combination of pepper and pigstye. Another author, Louise Beebe Wilder, thought Mr. Bowles's nose was "captious and too selective." In fact, the sweet scent of phlox readily floats on the air, with its musky base being caught only by sticking one's nose deeply into the flower head, for which there is no need or reason.

Modern hybridizing has brought many bi-color and suffused colors to phlox plants. 'Bright Eyes' is a pink flower with a crimson eye to each individual floret. 'Progress' is a light blue flower with purple eyes, and 'Franz Schubert' is a dreamy blend of mauve and lilac-pink with purple eyes.

Phlox are gross feeders and need a rich soil with lots of aged manure and compost, as well as peat moss and leaves mixed in. The masses of petals they can produce over such a long period of time require consistent water, and drought will shut down flowering.

Mildew was once a significant problem, but now many resistant hybrids are available ('David' is a white mildew-resistant cultivar). Mildew in phlox (and in Michaelmas daisies) is, strangely enough, encouraged by keeping the plants too dry. Water consistently and set the clumps with sufficient space for their expansion and to allow for good air circulation. If a plant develops mildew, it should be removed and only resistant plants kept in the garden. Bloom can be prolonged even further by pinching out the central flower head as soon as it begins to fade, a practice that will trigger new flower buds from side shoots.

Yarrow
The Plant of Tea and Sympathy

Still waters run deep with this useful plant that is familiar in most gardens for its practical features of drought resistance and long, six- to eight-week blooming period. But we have taken much for granted, for the friendly and self-effacing nature of yarrow belies its prominent profile in gardens past. If the accumulation of common folk names is any measure of yarrow's historical importance, what we have here is a supernova in the perennial borders.

The name yarrow is a scramble of the Anglo-Saxon word for the plant, *gearwe*, and the Dutch, *yerw*, neither of which offers any comfort to the casual reader. But the Latin name, *achillea*, sheds some light and refers to the Greek warrior Achilles who used the leaves to staunch the wounds of his soldiers during the Trojan War. The finely cut foliage inspired the descriptive term *millefolium*, or "thousand leaves." *Achillea millefolium* has been cultivated in gardens since before 1440 and was principally known as a blood-stopping wound-herb, as described in the country names staunchgrass, soldier's woundwort, herbe militaris, and nosebleed. The Scottish Highlanders still make a healing salve from it, and in a pinch, the leaves can be chewed to relieve toothache. It was also one of the herbs in very old days associated with the Evil One, hence the names devil's nettle and bad man's plaything. But in happier times yarrow has been substituted for hops in beer making (with improvement of the intoxication factor) and also brewed into a restorative and sympathetic tea for dispelling melancholy and severe head colds. The British author Marion Cran (*Joy of the Ground*, 1929) noted that yarrow grows in churchyards as a reproach to the dead, "who need never have come there if they had taken their yarrow broth faithfully every day while living."

A yarrow species not seen often enough is *A. ptarmica* 'The Pearl', also known as shirt-buttons, goosetongue, and sneezewort. It makes a cloud of small double flowers lasting the entire summer and is charming in a small vase by itself, or as filler in border bouquets. The country folk called it seven year's love, and Gloucestershire brides carried it in their bouquets with the hope of at least seven harmonious years. The leaves were dried and powdered for use as a snuff substitute for the working classes, engendering the name sneezewort (or old man's pepper), for it caused more sneezes

PLANT
Yarrow, *Achillea millefolium*,
A. filipendulina

OTHER NAMES
Thousand-seal, Nose-bleed, Staunchgrass, Soldier's Woundwort, Herbe Militaris, Knight's Milfoil, Devil's Nettle, Bad Man's Plaything, Old Man's Pepper, Field Hop

BLOOM
July to September

SIZE
Height 18 inches to 4 feet
(45 to 120 cm)

FORM
Open clumps

HARDINESS
Zone 4, hardy to –30°F (–34°C)

LOCATION
Full sun

SOIL
Average garden soil, well drained

WATER
Consistently moist in spring, tolerates short drought

PROPAGATION
Root division in spring or autumn, stem cuttings in summer

PLANT PARTNERS
Summer Phlox (*P. paniculata*),
Russian Sage (*Perovskia atriplicifolia*)

The distinctive flat heads of yarrow are ideal landing pads for bees and butterflies that love the nectar and bright colors. 'Cerise Queen' is one of the hybrids that break from traditional yellow.

than satisfaction. A dubious tea was made from the tarragon-scented leaves, but it seems not to have had a sleepy-time effect, and is described as similar to "a life on the ocean wave in rough and stormy weather."

Despite the heavily loaded past, yarrow is a fresh and motivating plant in the form of its new cultivars. In recent decades much work has been done to expand the color range and develop truly unique shades encompassing the deep reds ('Fire King' and 'Red Beauty'), dark pinks ('Rubra' and 'Cerise Queen'), and suffused art shades including 'Marmalade' (tawny orange and yellow), 'Old Brocade' (yellow, gold, and bronze), and 'Terracotta' (burnt sienna and pale yellow). The golden spectrum has been monopolized by another species, *A. filipendulina*, late to arrive from the Caucasus in 1804. Perhaps the most famous modern yarrow is 'Coronation Gold', a hybrid of *A. filipendulina* with corymb flower heads up to 5 inches (12.5 cm) across.

The yarrows are drought-hardy plants, but we are all greedy for the flowers and will get the most blossoms by providing consistently moist soil. The blooming period can be stretched by removing the spent flowers to encourage continuing production. Full sun and good drainage are required, for yarrow doesn't ever want soggy feet, and it prefers a lean soil with not too much rich food. The common yarrow (*A. millefolium*) is an ancient and pretty plant still sold at garden centers and likely to seed itself excessively about the garden. But the many named modern cultivars are better behaved and keep their place. Yarrows are attractive cut flowers, and Vita Sackville-West was fond of mixing them with tall branches of dill in a vase. They also retain their vivid colors when hung upside down to dry for winter arrangements. Yarrow has long been associated with Venus and the fates of loving couples. Country maids of marrying age would sew a handful of the leaves into a piece of flannel and place it under their pillows, repeating these words with hope to dream of their future husbands:

Thou pretty herb of Venus' tree,
    Thy true name it is Yarrow;
Now who my bosom friend must be,
    Pray tell thou me to-morrow.

HALLIWELL'S *POPULAR RHYMES*

6

LATE SEASON
blooms

"Wherever humans garden magnificently,
there are magnificent heartbreaks."

HENRY MITCHELL, THE ESSENTIAL EARTHMAN

Japanese Anemone
Lady Amherst Catches the Train

PLANT
Japanese Anemone,
Anemone × *hybrida*

OTHER NAMES
Autumn Anemone

BLOOM
July to October

SIZE
Height 2 to 4 feet (60 to 120 cm),
spread 2 feet (60 cm)

FORM
Large mound with tall branched
stems

HARDINESS
Zone 5, hardy to –20°F (–29°C)

LOCATION
Light shade to part sun

SOIL
Rich organic, with aged manure

WATER
Consistently moist, drought
diminishes bloom

PROPAGATION
Root division in spring or autumn

PLANT PARTNERS
Sneezeweed (*Helenium autumnale*),
Spiderflower (*Cleome hasslerana*,
annual)

Some plants come to us through such circuitous routes, improbable arrangements, and fortuitous accidents, they could just as easily have fallen by the wayside and we would be none the wiser. But fortunately the autumn-blooming Japanese anemone had an adventurous journey and is very much with us. A German doctor, Andreas Cleyer, living in Nagasake, Japan, where he represented the Dutch East India Company, first noticed it in 1682. Two centuries passed before the plant came to attention again, this time in China in 1844, discovered by Robert Fortune, who found it "in full flower among the graves of the natives, which are round the ramparts of Shanghae; it blooms in November when other flowers have gone by, and is a most appropriate ornament to the last resting-places of the dead."

Robert Fortune sent the plant home to England, where it was crossed with another anemone introduced by Lady Amherst from Nepal about 1829, the union of which produced a tall pale pink hybrid. That hybrid plant was grown in the gardens of the Frenchman M. Jobert at Verdun-sur-Meuse about 1851, and one season produced a single white root branch with pure white flowers. The white mutation was detached and propagated under the name of his little daughter, Honorine Jobert, and that is how we came to have one of the loveliest autumn-blooming flowers in the garden. But what if Robert Fortune's Chinese flower had died in transit? What if Lady Amherst had missed her train and never got to Nepal? What if M. Jobert had stayed late at lunch and not noticed the white stem? We can only thank the fates.

Many serendipitous circumstances have been to our advantage, and we now have many cultivars of this lovely plant which Vita Sackville-West says "comes as a salvation in this dreary, uninteresting time of the year." Japanese anemones have quite a long blooming period, and plants can be selected for early and late flowering to extend the season from August into October. 'September Charm' is the earliest, actually putting up its flower stems with tight buds in early August. It is also the only one of the group with spreading roots that will colonize moist soil, the others all being clump-forming. William Robinson (*The English Flower Garden*, 1883) had a strategy for extending the blooming season: "By having some on a north border, and some on a warm one, the bloom may be prolonged. The secret of success seems to be to prepare at first a deep

Japanese anemone 'September Charm' is earliest to bloom, starting in August for four to six weeks. Keeping the plants well watered is the way to extend bloom. This is one plant that doesn't benefit from deadheading. The fuzzy seed heads are ornamental into November.

bed of rich soil, and to leave the plants alone. They abhor frequent disturbance." If the seed heads of spent blossoms are left intact on the tall stems, they make a fine display for early winter, adding another four to six weeks of ornamental value.

Japanese anemones like a moist and organic bed with aged manure dug in for enrichment. They will sustain themselves through a drought in midsummer, but of course that will cut down on numbers of flowers produced, as it does with all perennials. But beyond keeping them reasonably moist, they are completely undemanding and no matter how many years they are in the garden, the first opening flowers always seem a pleasant surprise. The lovely 'Honorine Jobert' has white petals with golden central stamens on stems reaching 36 inches (90 cm). 'Queen Charlotte' is a semi-double pink flower, and 'Whirlwind' is a semi-double white.

Kamchatka Bugbane
The Dancers' Dilemma

PLANT
Black Cohosh, *Cimicifuga simplex,*
C. racemosa

OTHER NAMES
Black Snakeroot

BLOOM
August to September

SIZE
Height 3 to 4 feet (90 to 120 cm),
spread 2 to 3 feet (60 to 90 cm)

FORM
Tall erect branches with wands of
bloom

HARDINESS
Zone 4, hardy to –30°F (–34°C)

LOCATION
Partial shade to full shade

SOIL
Organic woodland soil

WATER
Consistently moist

PROPAGATION
Root division

PLANT PARTNERS
Hardy Aster (*Aster × frikartii*),
Pearly Everlasting (*Anaphalis
triplinervis*)

What mysteries are bred in the forest? The bugbanes are a family of herbal plants found in thin woods and shady places. They have been an important part of the herbal pharmacopeia for many years, originally used by Native American peoples and then enthusiastically taken up by Europeans. *Cimicifuga* takes its name from the Latin words *cimex*, "a bug," and *fugo*, "to repel," referring to its ability to repel insects. But its more important use was as an antidote for poisonous venom and treatment for rattlesnake bite, a frequent affliction in earlier centuries when frontiers were still to be explored. *Cimicifuga* later came into use as a cough suppressant for victims of whooping cough and also a treatment for children struck with St. Vitus' Dance, a convulsive nervous disorder, an outward sign of which was irregular jerking movement. The "dreaded dance" was accompanied by mental impairment, irritability, and depression, and sometimes occurred in epidemics among young people.

But for garden purposes, we are interested in bugbane's fuzzy wands of creamy flowers that rise in autumn, just in time to join ornamental cabbages, chrysanthemums, and Michaelmas daisies. The thick rosettes of dark green ferny leaves resembling astilbe foliage are attractive all summer, placed at the back of a border or mixed into a group of phlox. The plants have architectural value, and their slender form allows for a group of three to be placed together for strong impact in an otherwise uninteresting section of garden. When nights turn cool in late summer, Kamchatka bugbane sends up arching racemes crowded with small round buds opening to fuzzy white flower bursts that last for three to four weeks in the cooling air. 'White Pearl' has large, white bottlebrush-like flower stems and grows 3 to 4 feet (90 to 120 cm) high. The British hybrid 'Elstead' blooms very late, October to November, and is 4 to 6 feet (120 cm to 2 m) tall. An earlier summer-blooming cousin is *Cimicifuga racemosa*, black cohosh, and it is similar in most respects, but has larger flower wands and blooms from mid-July to mid-August.

The bugbanes enjoy a shady to part-sun position with organic woodsy soil that is enriched with aged manure and peat moss. They are dependent on consistent moisture and shouldn't be allowed to dry out; they will be happy wherever hostas and ferns are

Snakeroot or black cohosh (Cimicifuga racemosa) is the earlier bugbane, blooming midsummer with a tall meadow rue (Thalictrum). The later bugbane is C. simplex *'The Pearl', Kamchatka bugbane, blooming from August to frost.*

thriving. Grown in too much direct sunlight they will attempt to hide their blossoms and fail to stand straight. Give them the pleasure of a part-shade location with a little morning sun, or a corner in bright shade.

Michaelmas Daisies
The Horde of Barbarians

PLANT
Michaelmas Daisies,
Aster novi-belgii

OTHER NAMES
New York Aster, Starwort

BLOOM
August to October

SIZE
Height 10 to 40 inches (25 to
100 cm), spread 12 to 36 inches
(30 to 90 cm)

FORM
Dense clump

HARDINESS
Zone 4, hardy to –30°F (–34°C)

LOCATION
Full sun

SOIL
Average garden soil with good
drainage

WATER
Consistently moist, drought reduces
flowering

PROPAGATION
Root division and stem cuttings

PLANT PARTNERS
Toad Lily (*Tricerta hirta*), Acidanthera
(*Acidanthera bicolor*, tender bulb)

The autumn wood the aster knows,
The empty nest, the wind that grieves,
The sunlight breaking thro' the shade,
The squirrel chattering overhead,
The timid rabbits lighter tread
Among the rustling leaves.

DORA READ GOODALE

Every autumn the quiet green mounds of Michaelmas daisies give us such a shock when, seemingly overnight, they burst into the most outrageous bloom. Their brightness reminds us of the brazen azaleas of spring and pulls us back from packing in the garden prematurely. There is life there yet, and several weeks before the frost is in the ground. Gertrude Jekyll kept a separate garden for Michaelmas daisies which she visited daily, in October — "It is a delightful surprise to…come suddenly upon the Michaelmas Daisy garden in full beauty…where the flowers are fresh and newly opened, and in glad spring-like profusion, when all else is on the verge of death and decay, [it] gives an impression of satisfying refreshment that is hardly to be equaled throughout the year."

Asters take their name from the same Latin word, meaning "star," for reasons that all can see. They were in cultivation before 1596, but the association with Michaelmas was only made after 1752 with the adoption of Pope Gregory's revised calendar, causing Michaelmas Day (September 29) to fall 11 days earlier, at about the time asters come into bloom. Asters and daisies of all kinds belong to the Natural Order of the Compositiae, encompassing approximately 9,000 species (possibly a tenth of the whole vegetable kingdom). It's no wonder daisy-lovers have such confidence, with backing from numbers like that. William Sutherland (*Handbook of Hardy and Herbaceous Plants*, 1871) said most of these daisies were "a horde of barbarians which no sane gardener would admit within the boundaries of the refined circles of the cultivated Flora."

His sentiments were shared by the American botanist Asa Grey, who was frustrated by the frequent and uncontrollable spontaneous hybridizing of the plant — "Never was there so rascally a genus, they reduce me to despair." However, it was their ability to breed well that led to the many hundreds of cultivars largely developed from three species plants, *A. novi-belgii*, *A. novae-angliae*, and *A. laevis*.

In defense of these early asters, it can be said they were not much appreciated and seldom well cared for. It was William Robinson, the Victorian gardener who pulled gardening consciousness away from formal borders and back to a more natural style, who brought Michaelmas daisies to attention. "There is," he wrote, "a quiet beauty about the more select Starworts, which is charming in the autumn days, and their variety of colour, of form, and of bud and blossom is delightful." This new awareness set the tone for many decades and also helped establish the asters as garden plants for the autumn season. Almost a century later, the author H.E. Bates wrote, "When the michaelmas daisies are in full glory, heavy with butterflies, there are effects as of light seen through lace, of shadow heightening light and light deepening shadow."

Various sizes of Michaelmas daisies have been developed to suit every circumstance and can be grown in a teacup or a barrel. Their naturalism and relaxed style make it easy to use them in any bare patch of ground, and they make good fillers between summer-blooming perennials. Michaelmas daisies grow so easily and without special attention, you may forget where they are. But when all else is tatty and yellowing, suddenly they explode like a tide of colored stars in the border for another four weeks. The minis are no more than 10 inches (25 cm) high, and the largest can reach 4 feet (120 cm), and they bloom in the full range of autumn colors: rust, yellow, brick red, burgundy, violet-purple, mauve, rose, pink, and white. Asters will grow in moist garden soil, providing it has good drainage. If you remember to pinch back the growing tips of stems during June and July, the autumn plants will give double the amount of flowers.

Michaelmas daisies 'Snowbank' and 'Clara Curtis' defy the season by blooming in October. Pinching their growing tips back in June and July will double the flower buds.

Monkshood
The Plant of Witches' Flight

PLANT
Monkshood, *Aconitum napellus*

OTHER NAMES
Helmet Flower, Wolfsbane, Friar's Cap, Granny's Nightcap, Auld Wife's Huid, Captain Over the Garden, Chariot and Horses

BLOOM
August to October

SIZE
Height 3 to 4 feet (90 to 120 cm), spread 3 feet (90 cm)

FORM
Stiff erect stems

HARDINESS
Zone 4, hardy to –30°F (–34°C)

LOCATION
Shade to part sun

SOIL
Rich organic soil with aged manure

WATER
Consistently moist, won't tolerate drought

PROPAGATION
Root division, infrequently required

PLANT PARTNERS
Rose Mallow (*Hibiscus moscheutos*), Garlic Chives (*Allium tuberosum*, hardy bulb)

I have heard that Aconite
Being timely taken hath a healing might
Against the scorpion's stroke.

BEN JOHNSON, *SEJANUS*

Now here is a plant to be taken seriously, for it is strikingly beautiful and, having a poisonous nature, it can also strike you down permanently. Monkshood has been a familiar garden plant since the Middle Ages, enjoyed for its purple-blue blossoms on tall stems that command the garden in late summer, and also for certain unpleasant uses.

The plant earned the common name wolf's bane when it was used as a poison bait for wolves. William Turner wrote (1551), "This Wolf's bayne of all poysons is the most hastie poyson." Indeed, the gardening authors of all centuries have stories to tell of poor unfortunates, such as "a gentleman of France, who perished from the eating of only six or seven of the Blossoms in a Sallet." Linnaeus knew of a physician who could not convince his patient to consume the prescribed leaves of *Aconitum* and so, eating them himself, promptly dropped dead. And predictably there have been instances of spousal abuse too dreadful to mention. On the positive side, brandishing a stem of monkshood was thought to paralyze a scorpion, allowing one the opportunity to get out of the beast's way. A more interesting use for monkshood (recounted by Mrs. M. Greve, *A Modern Herbal*, 1931) was in combination with belladonna, as the two plants were said to be the ingredients in the witches' "flying ointments." Aconite causes irregular action of the heart, and belladonna produces delirium. These combined symptoms might give a sensation of flying and perhaps even produce a ghastly cackle.

But the negative aspects of this lovely plant must be seen in perspective, for we are well beyond the times when plants were indiscriminately eaten to test their effects. Many plants in perennial gardens have varying poisonous natures, and the important point is not to eat them. We have never found need to cook up lily-of-the-valley or delphiniums, and certainly wouldn't eat monkshood. The flowers have a most ingenious form made up of a lower pea-like section with a full hooded top, similar to a monk's hood and the obvious source of the plant's name. The upper hood is perfectly designed to accommodate the form of a bumblebee, its primary pollinator, and monkshood is not known to grow in parts of the world without native bumblebees.

The Latin name refers to the hill Aconitus in Pontica where Hercules fought with Cerberus. The Anglo-Saxons called it *thung*, their word for all plants in some respect injurious. But the Victorians had an elevated appreciation for the beautiful blossoms, and knew it as "chivalry" and "knighthood-errantry" in their language of flowers. Monkshood is a plant of chilly northern climates and has deepest blue color in cool and shady beds. It likes a rich soil with aged manure and peat moss, and is intolerant of drought. The Canadian plantsman Patrick Lima says, "If starved, overcrowded or dry at the roots, aconites lose their lower leaves and grow stunted and yellowish. Although a mulch is a help, it is no substitute for humusy soil from the start." Grown in brighter sun monkshood requires proportionately more water to perform well. The tuberous root system is slow to develop and best left undisturbed for several years.

The American gardener Helen Van Pelt Wilson thought *Aconitum napellus* indispensable in her garden and grew it with salmon and white phlox, 'Croftway Pink' bee balm, and *Eupatorium*, the Joe Pye weed. There are several cultivars of various heights and shades, and two beautiful ones are white 'Ivorine', which blooms in early summer, and pale blue *A. carmichaelii*, the azure monkshood, which blooms in August and September.

Aconitum tricolor *is a delicate white hood with touches of purple at the edges, a change from the usual deep blue varieties. Monkshood is strongly toxic and shouldn't be grown in food gardens or where small children roam. But it poses no problem for sensible adults who can enjoy it in the autumn garden.*

Obedient Plant
The Do-As-I-Say Flower

PLANT
Obedient Plant,
Physostegia virginiana

OTHER NAMES
False Dragonhead, Virginia Lion's
Heart

BLOOM
August to October

SIZE
Height 18 to 36 inches (45 to
90 cm), width 24 inches (60 cm)

FORM
Tall rigid stems

HARDINESS
Zone 4, hardy to –30°F (–34°C)

LOCATION
Part shade to full sun

SOIL
Average garden soil

WATER
Slightly dry to discourage spreading
roots

PROPAGATION
Root division in spring

PLANT PARTNERS
Azure Monkshood (*Aconitum
carmichaelii*), White Gaura
(*G. lindheimeri*)

Even if you have difficulty mastering the Latin name of this plant (*Physostegia*, which sounds like a sneeze), that's no reason to deny yourself one of the most playful garden perennials. Obedient plant offers an infrequent opportunity for adult gardeners to behave like children when no one is looking. *Physostegia* is a member of the mint family, as you might guess from its squarish stems and inclination to "run" and colonize new territory. The rigid stems carry vertical rows of small, close-set snapdragon-like flowers in shades of white and pale to purplish pink. They are long blooming and effortless to grow, and the fun part has to do with the precise vertical lines of flowers. Each little blossom is cleverly articulated at its base, and if gently pushed out of line it will stay where your finger leaves it. Small children and uninhibited adults love to realign the blossoms into their own design of nature.

The Greeks were being stuffy in labeling this winsome plant with a name based on the words *physa*, "a bladder," and *stege*, "a covering," referring to the inflated calyx that covers the fruit. (We don't care about the calyx, we just want to move the little flowers around.) The author H.E. Bates, who could be petulant in his opinions, enjoyed obedient plant because "you can twist its snapdragon flowers round into whatever position you like and make them stay there, thus doing a little show-off trick to your friends.…[It] is a plant for which I have never had more than a mild affection. Its white form, however, 'Summer Snow,' is a real enchantress.…It has the same refined appeal that I find in white violets.…" As with many gifted writers, contradiction was an interesting part of his character.

Obedient plant blooms for four to six weeks starting in mid-August. It grows well in average garden soil without fertilization, and moist earth will invite it to spread rapidly, sometimes an asset if you need to fill space. But it can easily be kept to one place, or significantly slowed down, by letting the soil be on the dry side. 'Pink Bouquet' is an insipid shade, but 'Rose Bouquet' is altogether better, a deeper color and taller plant growing to 36 inches (90 cm). 'Summer Snow' is sparkling white and not an aggressive spreader, growing to about 24 inches (60 cm). The most exciting color is 'Vivid', 24 inches (60 cm) high and a bright rose-colored flower that is excellent for cutting. 'Vivid' is later than 'Summer Snow' by two to three weeks, and having both in the garden extends the blooming period.

The obedient plants have an obliging nature above ground, but will eagerly follow their instinct to run in moist places. They are so engaging, why not give them a damp corner? 'Vivid' is the one we can't have enough of.

Showy Stonecrop
A Garden Seat

PLANT
Showy Stonecrop, *Sedum spectabile*

OTHER NAMES
Live-Forever

BLOOM
August to October

SIZE
Height 18 to 24 inches (45 to 60 cm), width 18 inches (45 cm)

FORM
Round clump

HARDINESS
Zone 4, hardy to –30°F (–34°C)

LOCATION
Part shade to full sun

SOIL
Average garden soil

WATER
Consistent moisture, tolerates short drought

PROPAGATION
Root division

PLANT PARTNERS
Heartleaf Bergenia (*Bergenia cordifolia*), Ornamental Kale (*Brassica oleracea*, annual)

The Victorian language of flowers gives stonecrop the characteristic of "tranquility," and that is a good choice. It has the look of age, an almost pre-historic presence, that sets it apart from other plants with more movement and flash. Its name is a classical reference for several succulent plants that hold water reserves in their fleshy leaves, and is taken from the Latin word *sedo*, "to sit." The descriptive term *spectabile* means "spectacular." And *Sedum spectabile*, at the height of its growth in autumn, does look like a charming vegetable-like stool one could sit on. Tall showy stonecrop, *Sedum spectabile*, is a fleshy-leaved plant with rosettes of blue-green buds that break ground in early spring and develop all summer. Stonecrop always looks the same; it never has a bad or good year, and performs consistently in dry or moist soil. It will grow in any soil that is well drained and appreciates some peat moss and leaves as soil amendments.

The buds of stonecrop appear early in spring and slowly rise through the season, turning pale green just before taking color late in summer. 'Autumn Joy' is the most dynamic cultivar and starts out as an attractive mound of pale pink that turns to rosy red and then burgundy. It is madly attractive to monarch butterflies and they will frequently mob the broccoli-like flower heads. Groups of three or five clumps of stonecrop make a good display, and it can also be used as a low hedge or high border edging. It is one of the most attractive plants in autumn and often is covered with hoar frost in morning light, one of the most beautiful sights in the autumn garden. If allowed to stand in winter, the stems and flower heads are quite ornamental in the snow. Stonecrop is attractive with ornamental grasses that have similar patterns of development and also is a good companion to large rocks.

S. spectabile 'Autumn Joy' is the most commonly grown of the tall stonecrops, but there are other attractive colors. 'Brilliant' has raspberry-carmine flowers and 'Meteor' is vivid pink. 'Star Dust' has white flowers that sometimes turn a very pale pink, and 'Variegatum' has cream flowers with variegated cream and green foliage.

'Brilliant' stonecrop has been spreading outward since early spring. When thick clumps overgrow themselves, cut leaning stems for vases. Allowing the plants to stand through winter makes an intriguing display of snow tuffets.

Sneezeweed
Helen's Nose

PLANT
Sneezeweed, *Helenium autumnale*

OTHER NAMES
Helen's Flower, False Sunflower, Swamp Sunflower

BLOOM
August to October

SIZE
Height 3 to 5 feet (90 to 150 cm), spread 18 inches (45 cm)

FORM
Tall branched stems

HARDINESS
Zone 3, hardy to –40°F (–40°C)

LOCATION
Full sun

SOIL
Rich garden loam with aged manure

WATER
Consistently moist

PROPAGATION
Root division in spring, stem cuttings

PLANT PARTNERS
Perennial Sunflower (*Helianthus* × *multiflorus*), Love-Lies-Bleeding (*Amaranthus caudatus*, annual)

Light-enchanted sunflower, thou
Who gazest ever true and tender
On the sun's revolving splendor.

CALDERON

(TRANSLATED BY PERCY BYSSHE SHELLEY)

Sneezeweed, *Helenium autumnale*, was named by the Greeks after Helen of Troy, famed for her supreme beauty, who fled to Troy with Paris and began an epic war. The common name is based on the use of the plant's dried leaves in making snuff, inhaled to cause sneezing that would supposedly rid the body of evil spirits (exiting through the nose). Sneezeweed is a member of the sunflower family and shares its brightness with many forms of wild daisy-like sunflowers that bloom in the wet autumn fields.

From late August to frost, sneezeweed flaunts fancy blossoms in colors of yellow, orange, red, and brown. The stiff branches carry hundreds of 2-inch (5 cm) flowers with high prominent crowns formed of a broad and dark disk surrounded by reflexed, brightly colored petals. They are elegant and bold flowers that look good in quantity, planted in crowded clumps in sunny spots with moist, rich soil. Sneezeweeds prefer moist soil and are even happy in wet garden spots, but will tolerate slightly dry circumstances if necessary. Large clumps can be divided after several years and the pieces set back in the soil 24 inches (60 cm) apart.

Good autumn companions are the dusty pink sedum 'Autumn Joy', white boltonia, and golden black-eyed Susan. Good color combinations of sneezeweed are 'Bruno', red and bronze flowers on 2- to 4-foot (60 to 120 cm) stems; 'Butterpat', all-yellow flowers growing to 3 feet (90 cm); 'Copperspray', with wide clusters of coppery red flowers; and 'Moreheim Beauty', an old-fashioned sneezeweed with rich brownish red flowers fading to burnt orange, on 3-foot (90 cm) stems.

The heleniums bring an unruly opulence to the late perennial garden with their velvety mahogany shades and prominent crowns, just when a burst of bloom is needed. They are plants of wet meadows and last longer with consistent moisture.

Wormwood
The Cinderella Plant

PLANT
Wormwood, *Artemisia stellerana*,
A. ludoviciana, *A. schmidtiana*

OTHER NAMES
Mugwort

BLOOM
August

SIZE
Height 12 inches to 4 feet (30 to
120 cm), spread 18 inches to 3 feet
(45 to 90 cm)

FORM
Sprawling clumps

HARDINESS
Zone 5, hardy to –20°F (–29°C)

LOCATION
Part shade to full sun

SOIL
Average garden soil, well drained

WATER
Moist, with good drainage

PROPAGATION
Root division and stem cuttings

PLANT PARTNERS
Strawflower (*Helychrysum
bracteatum*), Northern Sea Oats
(*Chasmanthium latifolium*,
ornamental grass)

Those who read the gardening magazines will know all the reasons for growing plants with silver-gray leaves — they are good foils to plants with deeper and brighter colors, cooling down hot tones and separating bold shades to prevent abrasive clashes. They can relieve the monotony of a solidly green setting and provide a subtle background to delicate pastel colors. But another reason not mentioned often enough is that they are usually the most elegant foliage in the garden, with more character, texture, and style than other greenery.

For many years artemisias were Cinderella plants, serviceable in the garden for specific tasks but never an ornamental feature. And that may have something to do with their scented herbal background, for most gray-leaved plants are members of complex herbal families, sharing a gene pool based in the dry and scruffy Mediterranean regions. French tarragon (*Artemisia dracunculus* var. *sativa*) is an artemisia associated with the kitchen. Southernwood (*A. abrotanum*) is an old species with many names — including lad's love, maiden's ruin, or old man — that has been grown in gardens for hundreds of years as a "supplemental" plant to frame or provide background to other plants of distinction. Rev. William Hanbury (*A Complete Body of Planting and Gardening*, 1770) wrote that southernwood "is usually planted by the outside of flower-gardens, for the improvement of nosegays, it being possessed of a strong odour, which to many, is very agreeable." Of course to some few unprepared for a scent of any kind, that was another reason to marginalize silver-leaved plants.

Fortunately, plant breeders came to their senses and dropped extensive marigold programs to have a look at what could be done with several artemisia species. And what they came up with was very fine. One grey-leaved plant with beautiful foliage is *A. stellerana* 'Silver Brocade', a low-growing groundcover under 12 inches (30 cm) high with silvery-green, deeply divided and rounded lobes that have the appearance of brocaded fabric. It is modestly expansive and a lovely edging plant or can spill over a stone retaining wall and deserves a place where it can be admired. *Artemisia ludoviciana* 'Valerie Finnis' is a leaved plant with stylized leaves growing to 24 inches (60 cm), and unlike other similar species, is not a rambunctious spreader. Another artemisia famil-

Artemisia *'Silver King' shows its elegance between cosmos, borage, and the flamboyant red* Amaranthus. *The final bells of* Nicotiana langsdorfii *are overhead.*

iar in gardens is *A. schmidtiana* 'Silver Mound', a feathery soft tuffet, 18 inches (45 cm) high and wide, of finely cut silvery-green foliage that looks and feels soft.

Artemisias like a sunny position, but will accept part shade locations with good drainage. Ordinary garden soil with low fertility suits them best, but drainage is the central issue so additional coarse sand added to their planting hole is a good investment. They require little maintenance beyond occasional dividing if plants die out in the center. Their odd yellow flowers are produced mid- to late summer, and can be removed if they detract from the foliage display.

APPENDIX A Plant Sources

Mail Order Plant Sources in Canada

Boughen Nurseries Valley River Ltd.
Box 12
Valley River, Manitoba
R0L 2B0
Tel. (204) 638-7618,
Fax (204) 638-7172
Hardy plants for Zones 1, 2, and 3.
Free catalogue.

Crescent Nursery
R.R. 4
Rockwood, Ontario
N0B 2K0
Tel. (519) 856-1000,
Fax (519) 856-2712
Perennials, hostas, daylilies, heucheras, pulmonarias. Free list.

Fraser's Thimble Farms
175 Arbutus Road
Salt Spring Island, British Columbia
V8K 1A3
Tel. and Fax (250) 537-5788
www.thimblefarms.com
Perennials, rare plants and bulbs.
Catalogue $3.

Gardenimport Inc.
Box 760
Thornhill, Ontario L3T 4A5
Tel. (905) 731-1950 and
800-339-8314
www.gardenimport.com
Unusual perennials. Catalogue $5 for 4 issues.

Hortico Inc.
R.R. 1, 723 Robson Road
Waterdown, Ontario L0R 2H1
Tel. (905) 689-6984,
Fax (905) 689-6566
www.hortico.com
Extensive perennial catalogue $3.

JDS Gardens
R.R. 4, 2277 County Road 20
Harrow, Ontario N0R 1G0
Tel. (519) 738-9513,
Fax (519) 738-3539
www.jdsgardens.com

Mason-Hogue Gardens
R.R. 4, 3520 Durham Road. 1
Uxbridge, Ontario L9P 1R4
www.masonhogue.com
Extensive perennials, hardy geraniums, drought-tolerant plants.
Catalogue $2.

The Perennial Gardens Inc.
13139 – 224th Street
Maple Ridge, British Columbia
V4R 2P6
Tel. (604) 467-4218, Fax (604) 467-3181
Herbaceous perennials, native flora.
Catalogue $5 for 4 issues.

The Plant Farm
177 Vesuvius Bay Road
Salt Spring Island
British Columbia V8K 1K3
Tel. and Fax (250) 537-5995
Hostas, daylilies, cranesbill geraniums. Catalogue $3.

Rainforest Nurseries Inc.
1470 – 227th Street
Langley, British Columbia Y2Z 1K6
Tel. (250) 530-3499, Fax (250) 530-3480
www.plantlovers.com
Uncommon perennials. Catalogue $5.

Red Lane Gardens
R.R. 3
Belfast, Prince Edward Island C0A 1A0
Tel. (902) 659-2478
www.peisland.com/day/lilies.htm
More than 600 daylily cultivars.
Catalogue $2, or download from Web site.

Strong's Daylilies
Box 11041
Stoney Creek, Ontario L8E 5P9
Tel. (905) 643-3271,
e-mail mstrong@cgocable.net
1,600 varieties of daylilies for northern
gardens. Catalogue $2.

Vesey's Seeds Ltd.
Box 9000
Charlottetown, Prince Edward Island
C1A 8K6
Tel 800-363-7333,
Fax (902) 566-1626
www.veseys.com
Spring perennial catalogue, free.

Mail Order Plant Sources in the United States

Bloomingfields Farm
P.O. Box 5
Gaylordsville, CT 06755-0005
Tel. (860) 354-6951
www.bloomingfieldsfarm.com

Kurt Bluemel
2640 Greene Lane
Baldwin, MD 21013-9523
Tel. (410) 557-7229
www.bluemel.com

Bluestone Perennials
7211 Middle Ridge Road
Madison, OH 44057
Tel. 800-852-5243
www.bluestoneperennials.com

W. Atlee Burpee & Company
300 Park Avenue
Warminster, PA 18991-0001
Tel. 800-888-1447
www.burpee.com

Busse Gardens
5873 Oliver Avenue, SW
Cokato, MN 55321-4229
www.bussegardens.com

Daylily Discounters
One Daylily Plaza
Alachua, FL 32615
Tel. (904) 462-1539
www.daylily-discounters.com

Heronswood Nursery
7530 NE 288th Street
Kingston, WA 98346
Tel. (360) 297-4172,
Fax (360) 297-8321
www.heronswood.com

**Klehm's Song Sparrow
Perennial Farm**
13101 E. Rye Road
Avalon, WI 53505
Tel. 800-553-3715,
Fax (608) 883-2257
www.klehm.com

Milaeger's Gardens
4838 Douglas Avenue
Racine, WI 53402-2498
Tel. 800-669-9956

Park Seed Company
1 Parkton Avenue
Greenwood, SC 29647-0001
Tel. (864) 223-7333
www.parkseed.com

Plant Delights Nursery
9241 Sauls Road
Raleigh, NC 27603
Tel. (919) 772-4794
www.plantdelights.com

Roslyn Nursery
211 Burrs Lane
Dix Hills, NY 11746
Tel. (631) 643-9347
www.roslynnursery.com

Thompson & Morgan
P.O. Box 1308
Jackson, NJ 0827-0308
Tel. 800-274-7333
www.thompson-morgan.com

Wayside Gardens
1 Garden Lane
Hodges, SC 29695-0001
Tel. 800-845-1124
www.waysidegardens.com

White Flower Farm
P.O. Box 50
Litchfield, CT 06759-0050
Tel. 800-503-9624
www.whiteflowerfarm.com

APPENDIX B Zone Guide

To ensure winter hardiness of plants in your garden, select perennials that are well within the maximum low temperatures in your region during the coldest winter months. There are several temperature zone maps used in North America and they are each slightly different. This creates some confusion for gardeners and the best thing to do is know what your lowest winter temperature is, and then compare that with the zone map in the book you are using. Below are the lowest winter temperatures and their zones, as determined on the USDA zone map, and these have been used throughout this book.

Zone 2	−50°F	−46°C
Zone 3	−40°F	−40°C
Zone 4	−30°F	−34°C
Zone 5	−20°F	−29°C
Zone 6	−10°F	−23°C
Zone 7	0°F	−18°C
Zone 8	10°F	−12°C
Zone 9	20°F	−7°C

INDEX

Achillea filipendulina, 125, 127
Achillea millefolium, 125, 127
Achillea millefolium 'Cerise Queen,' *126*
Achillea ptarmica 'The Pearl,' 125–127
acid soil, 3
Aconitum carmichaelii, 137
Aconitum napellus, 136–137
Aconitum tricolor, 137
ageratums, 103
alkaline soil, 3
'Allwoodii' pinks, 54
Althaea ficifolia, 111, 112
Althaea nigra, 110
Althaea rosea (Alcea rosea), 110–112
 alum root, 72, 88
Amaranthus, 145
American columbines, 51
Anemone blanda, 42–43, *43*
Anemone coronaria, 42
Anemone pulsatilla, 34–35, *35*
Anemone × *hybrida,* 130–131
Anemone × *hybrida* 'September Charm,' *131*
Anthemis tinctoria, 92–93, *93*
Antwerp hollyhocks, *111,* 112
Aquilegia alpina 'Hensol Harebell,' 51
Aquilegia canadensis, 51
Aquilegia chrysantha, 51
Aquilegia viridiflora, 51
Aquilegia vulgaris, 50, 51
Arends, George, 82
Artemisia abrotanum, 144
Artemisia dracunculus var. *sativa,* 144
Artemisia schmidtiana 'Silver Mound,' 145
Artemisia stellerana 'Silver Brocade,' 144
Artesmisia ludoviciana 'Valerie Finnis,' 144
Aster laevis, 135
Aster novae-angliae, 135
Aster novi-belgii, 134–135
Aster novi-belgii 'Clara Curtis,' 135
Aster novi-belgii 'Snowbank,' *135*
asters, 134
Astilbe chinensis, 82–83
Astilbe taquetii 'Superba,' 83
Astilbe × *arendsii,* 82–83
Astilbe × *arendsii* 'Ostrich Plume,' 83
astilbes, 47, 82–83, *83*
auld wife's huid, 136

autumn anemones, 130
azaleas, 3
azure monkshood, 137

baby's breath, 67, 84–85, *85*
bachelor buttons, 70
bad man's playthings, 125
balloon flowers, 98–99, *99*
Bartram, John, 86
Bates, H.E., 124, 135, 138
bee balms, 86–87, *87,* 109
beggar's baskets, 30
belladonna hybrids, 3, 136
bellflowers, 48–49, *49*
bergamot, 86
Bethleham sage, 30–31, *31*
black cohosh, 132–133, *133*
black-eyed susans, 100–101, *101,* 142
black Sampsons, 120
Blackmore and Langdon, 104
blanket flowers, 102–103, *103*
bleeding hearts, 46–47, *47*
bloody geraniums, 73
blooms
 deadheading, 5, 24–25
 delayed, 5
 extended, 5, 24–25
blue-bottle cornflowers, 70
blue cowslips, 31
blue fescue, 103
'blue funnel flowers,' 40
blue scillas, 58
blue violets, *39*
Boweles, A.E., 124
Bradbury, John, 120–121
bright shade, 16
British Flower Garden, The (Robinson), 54
British Herbal, The (Hill), 74
British Physician (Turner), 30
Buddleia davidii, 82
bugbanes, 132–133
butterfly bush, 82
butterfly delphiniums, 105

Campanula alliariifolia, 49
Campanula 'Blue Clips,' 103
Campanula medium, 49

Campanula persicifolia, 48–49
Campanula pyramidalis, 49
Canterbury bells, 49
captain over the garden, 136
Catalogue of Plants (Gerard), 76
Centaurea cyanus, 70
Centaurea montane, 70–71
Centaurea moschata, 70, 71
Cerastium tomentosum, 33
chalk plants, 84
chamomile, 92
de Charentonneau, Gaillard, 102
chariot and horses, 136
Chater, W., 112
checkerblooms, 118
Cheddar pinks, *53,* 54
cheeses, 110
chimney bellflowers, 49
Chinese bellflowers, 98
Chinese lanterns, 50
Chinese peonies, 68
Cimicifuga racemosa, 132–133, *133*
Cimicifuga simplex, 132–133
cinnamon ferns, 47
clay soil, 78
Cleyer, Andreas, 130
Coats, Alice M., 94, 102, 110
columbines, 50–51, *51*
common gypsyweeds, 94
Complete Body of Planting and Gardening, The
 (Hanbury), 63, 144
compost, 12
coneflowers, 103, 120–121, *121*
consistent watering, 19–20
Convallaria majalis, 60–62, *61,* 77
coral bells, 88–89
Coreopsis verticilata, 103
cornflowers, 70–71, *71*
Corydalis flexuosa, 79
Corydalis lutea, 78–79, *79*
Corydalis ochroleuca, 79
cottage pinks, 52–54
cowslips, 36, *37*
Cran, Marion, 125
cranesbills, 72
creeping baby's breath, 84

creeping phloxes, 32
creeping veronica, 94
cull me to you, 38
cutting back, 26
cutting off spent flowers, 5

daisies, 121, 134–135
Dane's flowers, 34
David, Père Armand, 82
Davidia involucrata, 82
David's harp, 76
'Dawn Ansell' primulas, *17*
daylilies, 55–57
deadheading, 5, 24–25
delayed blooms, 5
Delphinium ajacis, 104
Delphinium consolida, 104
Delphinium elatum, 104
Delphinium grandiflorum 'Blue Mirror,' 105
Delphinium staphisagris, 104
Delphinium × belladonna, 104–105
    delphiniums, 3, *18*
delphiniums, 3, *18*, 104–105
devil's nettles, 125
Dianthus gratianopolitanus, 53, 54
Dianthus plumarius, 52–54
Dicentra canadensis, 47
Dicentra cucullaria, 47
Dicentra eximia 'Luxuriant,' 47
Dicentra formosa, 47
Dicentra spectabilis, 46–47, *47*
Digitalis ferruginea, 90, *91*
Digitalis grandiflora, 90, *91*
Digitalis lutea, 91
Digitalis mertonensis, 91
Digitalis purpurea, 90–91, *91*
disease, 23
division, 26–27
Doctrine of Signatures, 30, *31*
Doronicum cordatum, 58–59, *59*
Doronicum plantagineum, 59
dove's foot, 72
dry shade, 17
Dutchman's Breeches, 47
dyer's chamomile, 92

Earl Grey tea, 86
Earth Smoke, 78
Easter flowers, 34
Echinacea augustifolia, 120
Echinacea purpurea, 103, 120–121, *121*
Echinops ritro, 106, *107*, 109

Eden; or a Compleat Body of Gardening (Hill), 34, 57, 104
English bulls-eyes, 100
English Flower Garden, The (Robinson), 113, 130
environmental stress, 18

fairy cups, 36
fairy gloves, 90
fall phloxes, 122
false dragonheads, 138
false sunflowers, 142
Feate of Gardening (Gardiner), 110
ferns, 47
fertilizers
    basic nutrients (N-P-K), 14
    forms of, 15
    mistakes with, 13
    nitrogen, 5, 14, 15
    phosphorus, 14
    potassium, 14
    timing of application, 13–15
    transplant solution, 21–23
field hops, 125
fig-leaved hollyhocks, *111*, 112
finger flowers, 90
flags, 74
fleur de luce, 74
Fleur de Lys, 75
flowering moss, 32
Flowers and Their Histories (Coats), 94
forget-me-nots, *37*, 58
Forsyth, Turid, 69, 93
Fortune, Robert, 130
foxgloves, 90–91, *91*
French tarragon, 144
friability, 6–7
friar's caps, 136
full sun, 16
Fumaria officinalis, 78

Gaillardia aristata, 102
Gaillardia drummondi, 102
Gaillardia pulchella, 102
Gaillardia × grandiflora, 102
Garden, The (Sackville-West), 34
garden phloxes, 122
Gardener's Assistant, The (Thompson), 46
Gardener's Dictionary, The (Miller), 78
Gardiner, John, 110
Geranium 'Johnson's Blue,' *73*
Geranium macrorrhizum, 72
Geranium robertianum, 73

Geranium sanguineum, 73
Geranium × oxonianum 'Claridge Druce,' 73
geraniums, 72–73, *73*
Gerard, John, 36, 54, 58, 67, 68, 74, 76
gillyflowers, 52
Glattstein, Judy, 59
globe thistles, 106, *107*, 109
Gmelin, Johann Georg, 98
golden coneflowers, 100
golden marguerites, 92–93, *93*
Goodyer, John, 92
gooseneck loosestrife, 108–109, *109*
granny-bonnets, 50
granny's nightcaps, 136
grass pinks, 52
green manure, 10–12
Greve, M., 60, 113, 136
Grey, Asa, 135
ground pinks, 32
Gypsophila elegans, 67, 84
Gypsophila paniculata repens, 84
Gypsophile paniculata, 84–85

Hanbury, William, 63, 144
Handbook of Hardy and Herbaceous Plants (Sutherland), 134
handkerchief trees, 82
hardiness zones, 4–5, 148
hearts-ease, 38
Helenium autumnale, 109, 142, *143*
Helen's flowers, 142
helmet flowers, 136
herb Peter, 36
herb Robert, 73
herb trinity, 38
Herbal (de Tournefort, J.P.), 50
Herball, or Historie of Plants (Gerard), 58
herbe militaris, 125
Hermerocallis esculenta, 57
Hermerocallis flava, 56, 57
Hermerocallis fulva, 55
Heuchera americana, 88–89
Heuchera americana 'Palace Purple,' 88, *89*
Heuchera sanguinea, 88–89
Hill, John, 34, 57, 74, 104
hollyhock rust, 112
hollyhocks, 110–112
hostas, 47
humus, 10–12

Indian blankets, 102
invasive root systems and seeds, 4

Iris florentina, 74
Iris foetidissima, 74
Iris germanica, 74
Iris pallida, 74
Iris siberica, 74–75
Iris siberica 'Atoll,' *75*

Japanese anemones, 130–131, *131*
Japanese loosestrifes, 108
Japanese tree peonies, 69
Jekyll, Gertrude, 37, 40, 62, 67, 84, 104–105, 112, 134
Jerusalem cowslips, 30
johnny-jump-up, 38
Joseph and Mary, 30
Joy of the Ground (Cran), 125

Kamchatka bugbanes, 132–133
key flowers, 36
kiss me in the garden, 38
knight's milfoils, 125

ladder-to-heaven, 60, 76
lady's locket, 46
lady's milk sile, 30
lamb's ears, 9
languid ladies, *41*
lark's heels, 104
larkspurs, 104
laughing parsley, 34
lavender, 9
Lawrence, John, 110–111
Lemoine, M., 68
lemon lilies, *56*
leopard's bane, 58–59, *59*
Lierval, M., 122
light requirements, 15–16
lily constancy, 60
lily-of-the-valley, 60–62, *61, 77*
Lima, Patrick, 39, 51
Linnaeus' theory, 100
live-forevers, 140
Lloyd, Christopher, 37, 48, 49, 99, 106, 115
love in idleness, 38
Love of Flowers, A (Bates), 124
low maintenance, *vs.* no maintenance, 2
lungworts, 30
lupines, 63–64, *64*
Lupinus albus, 63
Lupinus perennis, 63
Lysimachia clethroides, 108–109, *109*
Lysimachia nummularia, 108

Lysimachia punctata, 108

maintenance, 20
Malva alcea var. *fastigiata,* 113–114
Malva moschata, 113–114, *114*
'McKana's Giants' columbines, *51*
meadow anemones, 34
meadow rue, *133*
medieval herbalists, 30
meeting houses, 50
Mertens, Karl, 40
Mertensia ciliata, 41
Mertensia virginica, 37, 40–41, *41,* 58
Michaelmas daisies, 134–135, *135*
mildew problems, 123, 124
Miller, Jean (Jane), 40
miniature hollyhocks, 118
Mitchell, Henry, 46, 65
Modern Herbal, A (Greve), 60, 113, 136
Monarda didyma, 86–87, *87,* 109
Monarda fistula, 86
monkshood, 136–137, *137*
moss phlox, 32–33, *33*
moss pinks, 32
mountain bluets, 70
mountain phloxes, 32
Mrs. Glasse's Cookery, 68
muggets, 60
mugworts, 144
musk mallow, 113–114, *114*
Myosotis alpestris, 37, 58

New Herball, A (Turner), 34, 50
New York asters, 134
Nicotiana langsdorfii, 145
nitrogen, 5, 14, 15
'Nora Barlow' columbines, 51
nose-bleed, 125

obedient plant, 138, *139*
old maid's nightcap, 72
oldman's peppers, 125
Onoclea sensibilis, 47
opium poppy, 65
organic materials
    autumn amendment, 27
    clay soil, 8
    compost, 12
    decomposition, 11–12
    green manure, 10–12
    humus, 10–12
    planting holes, 21

renewal cycle, 21
sandy soil, 9
shade conditions, 17
sources of, 9
oriental poppy, 65–67, *66*
Origanum fistulosum, 86
orrisroot, 74
Osmunda cinnamomea, 47
oswego tea, 86
our-lady-in-a-boat, 46
our lady's gloves, 50
our lady's tears, 60
outlandish roses, 110
ox-eye chamomile, 92

'Pacific Giants' delphiniums, *18*
Paeonia hybrids, 68–69
Paeonia suffruticosa, 69
Paeonia tenuifolia, 69
pale thread leaf coreopsis, 103
pansies, 38, 58
Papaver bracteatum, 65–67
Papaver orientale, 65–67, *66*
Papaver somniferum, 65, 67
Paradisi (Parkinson), 92
Parkinson, John, 74, 76, 86, 92, 110
partial shade, 16
pasqueflower, 34–35, *35*
Paul's betony, 94
peach-leaved bellflower, 48–49
peonies, 3, 68–69
perennial cornflowers, 70–71
perennial geranium, 72–73
perennial phloxes, 122
perennial salvias, 115–117
Perenyi, Eleanor, 68, 106, 122
Perovskia atriplicifolia, 67
pest resistance, 3–4
pests, 23–24
pheasant's eye pinks, 52
Phlox 'Norah Leigh,' 124
Phlox paniculata, 32, 122–124, *123*
Phlox subulata, 32–33, *33*
phloxes
    moss, 32–33, *33*
    summer, 122–124
phosphorus, 14
Physostegia virginiana, 138
Physostegia virginiana 'Vivid,' 138, *139*
pinks, 52–54
plaintain leopard's bane, 59
plant sources, 146–147

planting, 21–23
Platycodon grandiflorus, 98–99, *99*
Pliny, 68
Polygonatum biflorum, 76–77
Polygonatum commutatum, 76–77
poppy anemones, 42
potassium, 14
prairie mallows, 118
primroses, 36
Primula polyanthus, 37
Primula veris, 36, *37*
Primula vulgaris, 36
primulas, *7, 17,* 36–37
pruning, 26
Prunus persica, 48
Puccinia malvacearum, 112
pug-in-a-pinner, 36
Pulmonaria augustifolia, 31
Pulmonaria saccharata, 30–31, *31*
Pulsatilla vulgaris, 34–35, *35*
purple coneflowers, 103, 120–121, *121*

rhododenrons, 3
roanokebells, 40
roast beef plants, 74
Robinson, William, 51, 54, 106, 113, 130–131, 135
Ronsdorf hybrids, 82
rosa ultramarinas, 110
Rudbeck, Olaf, 100
Rudbeckia fulgida var. *sullvantii* 'Goldsturm,' 100
Rudbeckia nitida 'Herbstonne,' 100
Rudbeckia occidentalis 'Green Wizard,' 101
rudbeckias, 100–101, *101*
Ruskin, John, 115
Russell, George, 63
Russian sage, 67

Sackville-West, Vita, 34, 48, 62, 90, 98, 122, 127, 130
sage, 115–117
Salvia × *superba,* 115–117
Salvia × *superba* 'Purple Rain,' *116*
salvias, 115–117
sandy soil, 9
scarlet bee balm, 86
Schenk, George, 62, 73, 94
scotch pinks, 52
Sedum spectabile, 140–141
Sedum spectabile 'Brilliant,' *141*
sensitive ferns, 47
shade conditions, 16–17
shameface, 72

shepherd's crook, 109
Sherard, James, 122
showy leopard's bane, 59
showy stonecrops, 140–141
Siberian delphiniums, 104
Siberian iris, 74–75
Sidalcea candida 'Bianca,' 118–119
Sidalcea malviflora, 118
Sidalcea neomexicana, 118
Sidalcea oregana, 118, *119*
'Sissinghurst White' pulmonaria, 31
Skipworth, Lady Jean, 40
small honesties, 52
snakeroots, 132
sneezeweed, 109, 142, *143*
sneezewort, 125–127
snow-in-summer, *33*
soaker hoses, 20
soil
    adaptability, 3
    amendment. *See* organic materials
    clay soil, 78
    fertility, 13–15
    friability, 6–7
    organic materials. *See* organic materials
    recognition of, 6–7
    sandy soil, 9
    types, 6–7
soldiers and sailors, 30
soldier's woundworts, 125
Solomon's seal, 76–77, *77*
sops in wine, 52
southernwood, 144
speedwells, 94–95, *95*
spotted dogs, 30
squirrel corn, 47
Stachys byzantina, 9
staking, 3
starworts, 134
staunchgrass, 125
Stavesaker, 104
Stevenson, Robert Louis, 60–62
stonecrops, *27*
storksbills, 72
summer phloxes, 122–124, *123*
sun conditions, 18
Sutherland, William, 134
swamp sunflowers, 142
sweet sultan, 70, *71*
Symons-Jeune, Herbert, 32–33, 122

'Telham Beauty' bellflower, 49

Thalictrum, 133
Theatrum Botanicum (Parkinson), 76
Theophrastus, 68
Thompson, Robert, 46
thousand-seal, 125
Tickenham Hill Violet Nursery, 39
de Tournefort, J. P., 50
Tradescant, John, 63–64, 86
transplant solution, 21–23
Travels into the Interior of America (Bradbury), 121
Turner, William, 34, 50, 136

Veronica filiformis, 94
Veronica gentianoides, 94
Veronica longifolia, 94, 95
Veronica repens, 94
Veronica spicata, 94, 95
Viola odorata, 38–39
Viola papilionacea, 39
Viola tricolor, 38, 39
violas, 58
violet sages, 115
violets, *7,* 38–39, *39*
Virginia bluebells, *37,* 40–41, *41,* 58
Virginia cowslips, 40
Virginia lion's hearts, 138

watering, 18–20
weeds, 25–26
Wharton, Edith, 48
white fumitory, 79
wild bee balms, 86
Wilder, Louise Beebe, 110, 124
'William Reeves,' *83*
willow bellflowers, 48
Wilson, Helen Van Pelt, 137
windflower, 42–43
windflowers, *43*
winter hardiness, 4–5
wolfsbane, 136
wolfsbohnes, 63
Wood and Garden: Notes and Thoughts, Practical and Critical, of a Working Amateur (Jekyll), 105
wormwood, 144–145, *145*
Writer in the Garden, The (Perenyi), 106, 122

yarrow, 125–127
yellow corydalis, 78–79, *79*
yellow fumitory, 78
yellow tuberoses, 55

zones, 4–5, 148